NEW LEFT DIPLOMATIC
HISTORIES and HISTORIANS

KENNIKAT PRESS

NATIONAL UNIVERSITY PUBLICATIONS

SERIES IN AMERICAN STUDIES

Under the General Editorial Supervision of

JAMES P. SHENTON

Professor of History, Columbia University

JOSEPH M. SIRACUSA

NEW LEFT DIPLOMATIC HISTORIES and HISTORIANS

The American Revisionists

NATIONAL UNIVERSITY PUBLICATIONS
KENNIKAT PRESS • 1973
PORT WASHINGTON, N. Y. • LONDON

Library of Congress Catalog Card No: 73-75575
ISBN: 0-8046-9037-5

Manufactured in the United States of America

Published by
Kennikat Press, Inc.
Port Washington, N.Y./London

For Sally
and Joseph Anthony

PREFACE

The purpose of this essay is to analyze recent trends in the writing of American diplomatic history, paying particular attention to the origin, nature and significance of the so-called "New Left" diplomatic historiography that began to take form during the 1960's. Whereas the radical political activists of the same period appear much more concerned with attempting to make history than with attempting to write it, the New Left diplomatic historians discussed in the pages that follow are a small but influential number of comparatively young, radical-minded members of the historical academy who have, during the decade of the sixties, more or less revived an essentially economic interpretation of American foreign policy. As employed here, "radical-minded" simply means advocating or favoring fundamental, non-destructive change in the American social structure.

Within this framework, the discussion will deal first with general characteristics of post-World War II American diplomatic historiography, with the aim of indicating New Left points of departure both from the preceding climate and from the thrust of historical scholarship; second, with an examination of the principal ideas and underlying assumptions of the single most important influence on the New Left, William

Appleman Williams; third, with various New Left interpretations of such critical points in United States diplomacy as the Spanish-American War, World War II and
the Cold War; fourth, and finally, with an assessment of
New Left impact on the history academy, mostly from
the vantage point of older, more traditional diplomatic
historians.

It should be noted that the results of Robert W.
Tucker's recent publication *The Radical Left and American Foreign Policy* (1971), several themes of which
parallel ideas developed in this analysis, appeared too
late for inclusion into this text. To have included them
at such a late date would have been a meaningless and
misleading gesture, inasmuch as the findings of each
study were reached independently. (The subject and
thesis of this study were conceived in the summer of
1970.) The reader of both essays will find that despite
some similar themes, such differences as purpose, control groups and general approach set them apart, making
each in its own way a special contribution to a better
understanding of the New Left historian. For this reason
the two essays should be considered complementary
rather than duplicative.

Finally, the writer wishes to record his intellectual
debt to Daniel M. Smith, without whose help and sug-
gestions this study never could have been completed.
The writer is indebted also to Robert A. Skotheim for
reading the original draft and for much helpful criticism. And lastly, the writer would like to thank Linda G.
Johnson for her tireless efforts and generous cooperation in the typing of the manuscript.

Joseph M. Siracusa

Andover, Mass.
August 14, 1972

CONTENTS

NEW LEFT DIPLOMATIC
HISTORIES and HISTORIANS

You quarrel with my conservatism, but it it is to build up one of your own; it will have a new beginning, but the same course and end, the same trials, the same passions.
Ralph Waldo Emerson, 1841

1. ORIGINS AND ANTECEDENTS OF THE NEW LEFT DIPLOMATIC HISTORIOGRAPHY

"In the late 1950's and increasingly in the 1960's," observed diplomatic historian Daniel M. Smith in 1970, "a New Left began to emerge with its own historical outlook on recent world events." Who were these New Left diplomatic historians? What was the purpose of their scholarship? What was the nature of the relationship between the New Left diplomatic historiography that emerged in the 1960's and the Realist School of American diplomacy, which to a certain extent had dominated the writing of American diplomatic history since 1945? What similarities, if any, did the New Left have to the Realists? What were their outstanding differences? Where did New Left historians go for their ideas? It is to these questions that this introductory comment will address itself.[1]

Who were these New Left historians? For one thing, they were young; for another, they were radical-minded. Smith characterized them in the following manner:

3

"Alienated by the smugness and alleged failure of an affluent middle class society, disillusioned by Cold War rhetoric, and appalled by the dangers of thermonuclear destruction, a number of mostly young intellectuals and scholars began to attack American foreign policy and to call for reducing or eliminating commitments abroad in order to concentrate on reform at home." Like an earlier generation of protesting historians who used revisionist interpretations "as weapons . . . in their battle against the establishment . . . and as lessons designed to influence American foreign policy," New Left scholars called into question not only the conduct of American diplomacy, which has been a subject of the history academy's ongoing criticism throughout the twentieth century, but also the validity of American society itself. The central hypothesis of this essay is that, by a vigorous critique of United States external relations, the New Left diplomatic historiography that emerged in the 1960's urged both implicitly and explicitly the replacement of America's capitalist political economy, which was considered structurally expansionist and counterproductive, with a nonexpansionist society, which presumably for the majority of New Left historians under consideration meant a near self-sufficient democratic socialism. To these writers American diplomacy assumed the form of a mirror in which to reflect the image that the failure of United States foreign policy, or its conceived failure, was nothing less than the failure of American society to come to grips either with private property or with the aftermath of the industrial revolution. In the sense that New Left historians used their scholarship as a vehicle of reform, their historiography may properly be called an historiography of protest.[2]

From another level of analysis the target of the New Left was the ethos of those traditional historians who, despite their individual differences, agreed that Soviet aggression lay at the heart of the Cold War. New Left historians no longer believed in the Manichean world of fundamental antagonisms and rival dreams perpetuated by such older historians as Samuel Flagg Bemis and Dexter Perkins, although the New Left, in its thoroughgoing condemnation of almost every aspect of American foreign policy, may have replaced what it regarded as the simplistic world of orthodox historians with one of its own. Age played an important role here. Although it is a truism that each generation writes its own history, the New Left's perspective differed somewhat from that of its predecessor. The new revisionists, who were generally born in the 1930's and had come to intellectual maturity in the 1950's and 1960's, developed a view of the contemporary world in which the excesses and mistrust engendered by "free world" diplomacy appeared little different from the assumed evilness of the "communist world." As it was put by a student of American history who ironically had contributed much to the vision of mortal combat with the Soviets: "As the Cold War had begun to lose its purity of definition, as the moral absolutes of the fifties became the moralistic clichés of the sixties, some have begun to ask whether the appalling risks which humanity ran during the Cold War were, after all, necessary and inevitable, whether more restrained and rational policies might not have guided the energies of man from the perils of conflict into the potentialities of collaboration." More than any other single factor, one suspected that it was this revulsion to the Cold War climate of opinion that inspired the majority of New Left dissenters. Unlike other forms of revisionism resting on entirely new evidence, New Left revisionism rested, for the most part, on a rather different perception of the world and of America's role in it. Perhaps James A. Johnson best summed up the attitudinal change when he noted that "the most basic change in the perception of international reality in the last eighteen years is that the delineation of the world into the 'good guys' and the 'bad guys' on a one-dimensional scale is impossible." In sum, for the New Left, as well as for an increasing number of clearly non-Left scholars and diplomats, the previously perceived threat of an international Communist attempt to take over the "free world" had by the 1960's an unreal quality about it.[3]

Much of the confusion surrounding the origin of the new revisionism stemmed from the often repeated approach of explaining the rise of New Left historiography, in general, almost solely in terms of a reaction against "consensus" historiography, both the definition and characterization of which had been discerned by John Higham. But so far as the New Left diplomatic historiography of the sixties was concerned, the consensus interpretation, or the muting of conflict and diversity in explaining change, had little or no applicability. While one may rightly speak of a prevalent consensus among historians in discussing domestic issues, it seems markedly clear that there has been a great deal of dissent among practitioners of United States diplomatic history over foreign affairs since at least the beginning of the twentieth century. New Left historians unfortunately contributed to their own stereotype by defining themselves and their work in terms of reaction against a consensus climate of opinion. In the early 1960's, explained Barton J. Bernstein, "from historians, and particularly from younger historians, there began to emerge a vigorous criticism of the historical consensus," although it was by no means certain what the phrase meant.

New Left literature itself revealed a multilayered

Procrustean-like consensus that operated usually at more than one level of analysis. Throughout his unrelieved critique of America, Gabriel Kolko found a pervasive domestic consensus in which corporate capitalism defined "the essential preconditions and functions of the larger social order, with its security and continuity as an institution being the political order's central goal in the post-Civil War experience"; in a somewhat different context, however, Kolko focused on the nation's foreign policy consensus, which he called "Hullian' and defined as a rationalized world order in which goods and services could flow freely back and forth over national boundaries.

Walter LaFeber viewed the American consensus in a later and different light. Suggesting that Americans were reaching out for a consensus rather than always having had one, LaFeber contended that an ideological consensus finally was obtained by this nation in the presidential campaign of 1956, at which time "a small majority of Americans preferred Democratic domestic policy, but a larger majority supported Republican foreign policy." Whether discussing historical, domestic or foreign policy consensus, New Left historians' differences in this respect simply highlighted the fact that however strong the case for a domestic political consensus, the concept of a foreign policy consensus defied simple explanation. It is ironic that in their attempt to plumb alleged consensual sources of United States foreign policy the new revisionists created a unanimity of American views and opinions that may never have existed.[4]

The New Left's general approach to foreign policy further suggested an analysis of American diplomacy that was neither new nor, for that matter, very far left. Scott Nearing, for example, fifty years ago applied a far more vigorous leftist critique to what he then imagined to be the tragic implications of an inexorably expanding American empire. Adumbrating Gar Alperovitz's criticism of "atomic diplomacy" by twenty-five years, British physicist P. M. S. Blackett concluded "that the dropping of the atomic bomb was not so much the last military act of the Second World War, as the first act of the cold diplomatic war with Russia in progress." In like manner, the supposedly controversial thesis of Les K. Adler and Thomas G. Patterson that "Americans both before and after the Second World War casually and deliberately articulated distorted similarities between Nazi and Communist ideologies, German and Soviet foreign policies, authoritarian controls and trade practices, and Hitler and Stalin," had clearly been discerned by contemporaries in 1946, when, it appeared evident to at least one British Labor Member of Parliament that the point of similarity lay only in the dynamism of two fundamentally different totalitarianisms. The work of these and other earlier, hostile critics of post-World War II American foreign policy indicated that New Left historians, despite shrillness of voice and apparent novelty, travelled clearly marked paths. As all historical debate is rooted in the past, what they had done was rediscover or revive earlier critiques and of course write on them more extensively and passionately.[5]

More importantly, the new revisionism drew heavily on analyses provided by the so-called Realist School of Thought, a broadly-based criticism of American foreign policy that had informed much of United States diplomatic historiography since 1945. With reference to twentieth-century foreign policy in general and Cold War history in particular, the Realist School of American diplomacy, together with the historical debate it engendered, served as a point of departure for the majority of the New Left. This being the case, it may be useful to examine the assumptions and principal themes of this particular historiographic trend.

Since World War II there has been a continuous policy debate in this country between the advocates of idealism and the advocates of realism. Focusing on the idealistic or "soft" side of American diplomacy, a number of critics including scholars and diplomats such as Hans J. Morgenthau and George F. Kennan expressed anxious concern over the national tendency to perceive external affairs from an overly moralistic viewpoint and to turn wars into great crusades to remake the international order. The basic assumption of the Realist was that man's capabilities in this world necessarily were finite, and that power, controlling the minds and actions of others, was the engine of human motivation. For example, in *Scientific Man vs. Power Politics* (1946), an outgrowth of a previous lecture inspired by the fall of France, Morgenthau contended that practitioners of liberal foreign policy often mistook the basic assumption of political life, power, for a defect to be treated, failing to recognize "that power politics, rooted in the lust for power which is common to all men is . . . inseparable from social life itself." Warning that efforts expended to eliminate the will to power in international politics were the pursuit of a will-o'-the-wisp, Morgenthau suggested all man could hope to achieve in this area was a lessening of the destructiveness of power politics. Americans who refused to face up to the harsh reality of international life simply deluded themselves. He added, in a manner reminiscent of Reinhold Niebuhr, "There is no escape from the evil of power, regardless of what one does. Whenever we act with reference to our fellow men, we must sin, and we must still sin when we refuse to act." That Morgenthau had created a theory of causation appropriate to an existential hell can hardly be doubted.[6]

In terms of historical interpretation, Morgenthau perceived three major periods of American foreign policy. The first, corresponding to the first decade of the United States as a nation, was the realistic, essentially thinking and acting in terms of power and best represented by Alexander Hamilton; the second, corresponding to the period from the beginning of the nineteenth century to approximately the Spanish-American War, was the ideological, thinking in terms of moral principles but acting in terms of power and best represented by Thomas Jefferson and John Quincy Adams; the third was the moralistic, both thinking and acting in terms of moral principles and best represented by Woodrow Wilson and Franklin Roosevelt. This last period particularly interested Morgenthau, who contended that during the Spanish-American War era intoxication with moralism became the dominant substitute for political thought. Accordingly, Morgenthau began his assault upon twentieth-century American diplomacy with William McKinley. "At the beginning of the third period," ran the argument, "McKinley leads the United States as a great power beyond the confines of the Western Hemisphere, ignorant of the bearing of this step upon the national interest, and guided by moral principles completely divorced from the national interest." From this point Morgenthau took McKinley at his word and accepted his explanation that God had told him to annex the Philippines, a strategic blunder of the first magnitude. Thus disposing of McKinley, he turned his fire upon Woodrow Wilson's conduct in World War I. Morgenthau held that Wilson never was capable fully of understanding when the national interest was directly menaced, and that he never was capable of perceiving the threat in other than moralistic terms. In the end, Morgenthau concluded, "It was only the objective force of the national interest, which no rational man could escape, that imposed the course of America's mortal danger upon him as the object of his moral indignation."[7]

In regard to Franklin D. Roosevelt and the coming of World War II, Morgenthau suggested that the German threat again was perceived and acted upon in Wilsonian terms. Fortunately, however, "The moral postulates inspiring the administration of Franklin D. Roosevelt happened to coincide with the exigencies of American national interest . . . again, as in the case of Jefferson and of Wilson in 1917, due to the impact of a national emergency upon innate common sense, and to the strength of a national tradition that holds in its spell the actions of even those who deny its validity in words."

Furthermore, blinded by the glare of Hitlerism throughout the war years, few Americans bothered to deal with the then-forming postwar balance of power. In fact, noted Morgenthau, the idea of World War II being fought in view of a new balance of power shortly to be established occurred only to Winston Churchill and Joseph Stalin. When the enormity of the Soviet threat finally was recognized, and almost always for the wrong reasons, "it was with deeply and sincerely felt moral indignation that the Western world, expecting a brave new world without power politics, found itself confronted with a new and more formidable threat to its security as soon as the old one had been subdued." Morgenthau never questioned what he perceived as the gravity of the situation. The Russian objective was clear and unmistakable: domination of Eastern Europe and penetration as far as possible into Central and Southeastern Europe. In assessing the nature of Soviet aggression in ideological terms, as Morgenthau believed the Truman policy of containment did, the majority of Americans overlooked the obvious fact that Soviet "objectives expressed the traditional national interest of Russia in Europe as clearly as opposition to both of them was required by the traditional American national interest in the maintenance of the European balance of power." To this end, Morgenthau declared that both in Europe and in Asia the principal aim of United States foreign policy was the restoration of the balance by means short of war.[8]

Like Morgenthau, George F. Kennan perceived the most serious fault of America's past policy formulation as something he called "the legalistic-moralistic approach to international problems." It had in it, according to Kennan, "something of the old emphasis on arbitration treaties, something of the Hague Conferences and schemes for universal disarmament, something of the more ambitious American concepts of the role of international law, something of the League of Nations, something of the Kellogg Pact . . . something of the belief in World Government. But it is none of these entirely." What was it then? "It is," wrote Kennan to the point, "the belief that it should be possible to suppress the chaotic and dangerous aspirations of governments in the international field by the acceptance of some system of legal rules and restraints." Within this context Kennan found the landscape of twentieth-century American diplomacy in a state of ruin.[9]

According to Kennan in a highly influential collection of essays published in 1950, the decision to go to war with Spain seemed attributable to the agitated state of public opinion, to the rhetoric associated with a year of congressional elections, to the jingoism of a certain section of the American press, and, finally and perhaps most importantly, to the tremendous political pressures exerted on President McKinley. With respect to economic motives, Kennan said, "It is an interesting fact, incidentally, that financial and business leaders, allegedly the instigators of war, had no part in this and generally frowned on the idea of our involvement in the hostilities." So far as acquisition of an overseas empire was concerned, Kennan attributed it to an aroused nationalism, to "the fact that the American people of the day, or at least many of their most influential spokesmen, simply liked the smell of empire and felt an urge to range themselves among the colonial powers of the time, to see our flag flying on distant tropical isles, to feel the thrill of foreign adventure and authority, to bask in the sunshine of recognition as one of the great imperial powers of the world." Moreover, Kennan's treatment of the Hay open door notes underscored the "innocence" motif that marked much of the Realist interpretation of pre-World War II diplomacy. Kennan maintained that Hay had no idea of what was happening, never knew what he signed, and hardly had a thought about its implications." "It was not," according to Kennan, "a formula which Hay had drafted. There is no evidence that he understood fully its practical significance." In fact, all that Hay knew for certain was that the formula had a high-minded and idealistic ring about it and that it would be good for domestic consumption.[10]

Kennan, like Morgenthau, condemned "moralistic-legalistic" underpinning of Wilsonian foreign policy. Although Kennan conceded it was probably logical that defense of their neutral rights was the only interest in World War I Americans were inclined to recognize for a long time, he found it difficult to understand how they could have attached so much importance to those rights. For, as he went on to say, "they irritated both belligerents and burdened our relations with them, and I find it hard to believe that they involved our national honor." Kennan said that, failing utterly to recognize destruction of imperial Germany as a great power would shatter the equilibrium of Europe, Wilson or at least the Wilsonian logic demanded a total victory over the enemy. Accordingly, Germany became the devil incarnate, and the Allies went about the task of making the world safe for democracy. Instead of peace, the map of Europe had been rearranged for the next war. Kennan wrote, "This was the kind of peace you got when you allowed war hysteria and impractical idealism to lie down together like the lion and the lamb; when you indulged yourself in the colossal conceit of thinking you can suddenly make international life over into what you believed to be your own image; when you dismissed the past with contempt, rejected the relevance of the past to the future, and refused to occupy yourself with the real problems that a study of the past would suggest." From the Kennan viewpoint, the Wilsonian legacy unfortunately was passed on to Franklin D. Roosevelt.[11]

Kennan assumed that the basic cause of World War II was a defense of the Western democracies against a virulent totalitarianism. Kennan noted that despite the totalitarianism of the Soviet regime there could have been no prompt victory over Nazi Germany without the help of the Russians, a lesson not lost on Soviet leaders. For Soviet assistance, he added, "the Western democracies would have to pay heavily in the military consequences of the war and in the demands that would be raised at the peace table." Here lay the origin of the Cold War. In the passions generated by the struggle against Germany, Americans tended to forget that the Soviets had had no desire to fight on the side of the Allies and that only Hitler's attack on the Soviet Union made them willy-nilly partners. The destruction of Nazi Germany in turn allowed the Soviets to secure hegemony over postwar Eastern Europe, a need inherent both in Communist ideology and in Russia's search for security. It was then, remarked Kennan, "that many Americans became aware, for the first time, of the horrible reality of the postwar world—of the fact that this earnest and upright partner was not there at all, and that in his place there was only another one of those great inexplicable monsters, more formidable this time than all the others, sitting astride the resources of half the world and the prostrate peoples of Eastern Europe and China."[12]

Emerging from a world war that had wrought unprecedented death and destruction, Americans recoiled from the possibilities that even greater death and destruction lay ahead and that the engines of destruction which had been manned by the Nazis now were being manned by what were believed to be equally ruthless Soviets. Whether the Soviets were then prepared to embark on a course of world conquest was beside the point; what was important was that the American perception of just such a possibility never was far from the collective mind. Americans were not in complete agreement as to what to do about it. Such critics of Realism as Frank Tannenbaum, who held that a foreign policy based on power politics and a balance of power concept flew in the face of the traditional American commitment to equality of states, both large and small, contended that the proponents of idealism in foreign policy were prepared to resist to the death any effort to subvert the world to totalitarianism and that they, unlike the Realists, would in no way "bargain with it at the expense of other people and to the destruction of that sense of human integrity and national morality which is part of the substance of our very being." In a less ambitious manner, such

Realists as Kennan, regardless of the subsequent controversy over the means he implied in his famous "X"
article, sought to contain, and hopefully push back, the
Soviets from their forward positions, having not the
slightest doubt that retraction of Soviet power from its
then-bloated and unhealthy state was essential to a
stable world order. Whichever position one took, and
both were fraught with danger, the U.S.S.R. was uniformly designated as the potential aggressor and dis-
rupter of world peace.[13]

Despite their shared dislike of the surfeit of idealism
supposedly evidenced in Wilsonian-Rooseveltian foreign policy, New Left historians rejected outright the
Realists' "legalistic-moralistic approach to international
problems" as an inadequate concept in interpreting
American diplomatic history, especially as it applied to
the late nineteenth and twentieth-century period. To
be certain, American self-righteousness and perhaps
excessive idealism, usually in the sense of a self-appointed
mission to remake the world into its own image, loomed
large in the story, but only in a secondary manner. In
response to the Realist's criticism of the ideological or
"soft" side of American external affairs, which too often
took rhetoric at face value, the new revisionist largely
concerned himself with the economic or "hard" side.
The New Left argument, simply stated, is that United
States foreign policy should and could be best interpreted
as an ongoing function of America's capitalist political
economy, a political economy, furthermore, whose structural dynamics required both ever-expanding markets
for a continuous flow of surplus goods and capital and
easy access to raw materials in a freely trading world.
Any nation, system or political arrangement threatening
that goal became, by America's definition of itself and
its role in the international community, an object either
to be co-opted into acquiescence or otherwise eliminated.

To say this, however, was not to disparage ideological-strategic factors, for they too played an important and, sometimes, a great role. Their significance, the New Left thesis continued, was that they were unintelligible considered apart from the requirements, or what were imagined to be the requirements, of a post-Turnerian industrial society which made the world's market place the last frontier. In this manner, by assuming that foreign policy derived rationally, almost mechanistically, from the nation's political economy, New Left historians sought to deprive United States diplomatic history of any of its putatively adventitious character. What previously had been considered irrational and innocent now became rational and calculated. What previously had been naïve and self-explanatory rhetoric now became the typology of empire. Mistakes, chance and passions were reduced to design or dissimulation. The New Left, in effect, turned the Realist critique inside out.

McKinley's decision to go to war, for example, appeared to the revisionist not the decision of either a weak or ignorant politician, but instead, according to William Appleman Williams, the dean of the New Left, "one of the most striking displays of presidential nerve and finesse in the nation's history." The acquisition of an overseas empire no longer seemed the impetuous act of nationalists who enjoyed the smell of empire, but rather, in Walter LaFeber's view, "a natural culmination" of the American industrial revolution. The naïve idealism and apparent mindlessness of Hay's open door notes became, in the view of Thomas J. McCormick and Lloyd C. Gardner, a carefully prepared plan "of acquiring the economic fruits of empire without extensive political-military responsibilities and burdens," in every sense "the foreign policy of a confident industrial power."[14]

Much of the dreamlike idealism that supposedly in-

formed Wilsonian foreign policy assumed a new character. The ultimate goal of Wilson's foreign policy, which
Kennan had described as the misguided "belief that it
should be possible to suppress the chaotic and dangerous
aspirations of governments in the international field by
the acceptance of some system of legal rules and restraints," appeared in N. Gordon Levin's judgment as
"the attainment of a peaceful liberal capitalist world
under international law, safe both from traditional imperialism and revolutionary socialism, within whose stable
liberal confines a missionary America could find moral
and economic pre-eminence." The method chosen by
Wilson and his followers to realize this objective was the
League of Nations. Carl P. Parrini wrote, "in their view
such a league could force disarmament and write open
door rules to govern the political economy." Moreover,
opponents of the League, in much the same way as opponents of acquiring the Philippines before them, were
portrayed as Americans differing from one another over
means not ends. In this sense the Leagues' opponents,
wrote Parrini, "to a greater or lesser extent concluded
that Wilson's Article 10 of the League of Nations was too
inflexible to achieve real disarmament or generate the
pressure to widen successively the application of the
open door to even larger areas of the world."[15]

Likewise, United States participation in World War II
became something more than just the defense of Western democracies against the evilness of totalitarianism
in general and Hitlerism in particular. Hitler's threat to
America, contended revisionist Lloyd C. Gardner, "was
a total challenge certainly, but it was not the existence
of Nazism per se that made World War II and America's entrance into the struggle inevitable; rather, it was
the expansion of the system." Failing to check axis
expansion, which had its own dynamic requirements,

American policy makers decided to resist. In this manner, New Left historians such as Robert Freeman Smith jettisoned the conventional "view of a somewhat befuddled, defensive United States facing a world of predatory aggressors, and instead present [ed] the United States as a rather imperial-minded power with ambitions and goals which on the whole are rather similar to those of most powers."

Finally, the Cold War, which Realists previously had depicted as the outcome of the American response to a putatively aggressive Soviet foreign policy which sought to obtain traditional Tsarist objectives in Eastern and Central Europe assumed the appearance, according to the New Left model of United States diplomatic behavior set up by David Horowitz, of "a war for the American frontier." Conceding Realists' arguments that the disappearance of the axis powers necessarily made the United States and the U.S.S.R. principal contestants in the newly emerging postwar balance of power, New Lefters such as Gardner relentlessly insisted "that the United States was more responsible for the *way* in which the Cold War developed." The issue was simple: America wanted an open world; the Soviet Union did not. Put another way but equally succinctly by Gabriel Kolko, revisionist par excellence, "It [the United States] wished to sell." In the Cold War, as in other critical periods in American diplomatic history, the New Left repeatedly emphasized that although ideological considerations undoubtedly were important, economic considerations were determinative. LaFeber declared that of all the forces influencing American decision-making in the post-World War II period, "Policy-makers could consider the economic the most important . . . a not unreasonable conclusion given the national crisis endured in the 1930's." It was not surprising, LaFeber concluded, that the abso-

lute prerequisite of United States foreign policy became
the free flow of exports and imports in a nonrevolution-
ary world, the blind pursuit of which led straight to the
jungle of Vietnam. That Vietnam has few economic
resources to offer makes the American presence there
no less rational in the New Left schema. Although
"Vietnam itself has relatively little value to the United
States," argued Kolko perversely, "[it] is all the more
significant as an example of America's determination to
hold the line as a matter of principle against revolutionary movements." In any case, according to the new
revisionism, there was nothing particularly evil about the
intention of American policy makers; they almost always
thought they were pursuing peace. And despite the fact
they could have chosen otherwise they seldom did. In
point of fact what was evil was the social system that
generated that policy.[16]

Having discussed the New Left point of departure
from the preceding Realist School of American diplomacy, the question rises as to whom New Left diplomatic historians have gone for their ideas, the "logic"
of the evidence to the contrary notwithstanding. The
answer to this question provides the final clue in explaining the emergence of a revisionist opposition to mid-
twentieth-century American foreign policy.

The New Left's nonliving heroes included among
others Charles Austin Beard and Karl Marx. New revisionists' debt to Beard was substantial both for an
exclusively American interpretation of industrial imperialism and for a basic approach postulating the axiom
that foreign policy and domestic policy were aspects of
the same thing. William Appleman Williams, of whom
more later, acknowledged his intellectual debt to Beard
unequivocally. "It . . . seems appropriate, in view of all
the bigoted and career building attacks, acts of purifi-

cation, and even smart aleck criticism," wrote Williams, "to acknowledge formally my respect for and indebtedness to Charles Austin Beard." Others such as LaFeber did so implicitly. For example, in his review essay of R. W. Van Alstyne's *Rising American Empire* (1960), LaFeber noted that it was indeed "odd that historians who worry most about keeping the American story clean for Cold War purposes and free from Beardian interpretation are reluctant to give their ancestors credit for brilliant debates, detailed blueprints, and the sound structuring which created one of the largest and most successful empires in world history."

New Left foreign policy goals manifested an unmistakable Beardian touch. Beard's conclusion, in 1934, regarding the necessity of eliminating outward thrusts and being an exemplary power, the true national interest, could have been written yesterday. Similar also to the New Left's general thesis was Beard's belief that it would be most unwise for the United States to depend on foreign markets as the only outlet for its surplus goods and capital. More importantly perhaps, the New Left's contention that national foreign policy derived rationally and logically from America's capitalist political economy bore a marked resemblance to Beard's earlier analysis. After once dismissing as childish the hypothesis that evil politicians and bankers conspire to make wars, an hypothesis which he, in part, unfortunately revived in his last studies of Rooseveltian foreign policy, Beard attributed the cause of war in a capitalist society to a simple dynamic inherent in the capitalist system. In a machine society, argued Beard, there were usually more goods to sell than people at home were willing to buy. Advocating mandatory embargo laws, Beard advised Americans to look inward in much the same manner as new revisionists would thirty-five years later. "I think,"

wrote Beard, "we should concentrate on tilling our own
garden. It is a big garden and a good garden, though
horribly managed by our greedy folly." Beard's view of
America in the 1930's together with his solution to the
problem, must have suggested to the New Left a haunt-
ingly familiar picture. Like the radical historian of the
1960's, Beard, was "appalled by the sight of slums, un-
employed millions, poverty, and degradation on the one
side and the immense productive potentials of agricul-
ture and industry in America"; again like the radical
historian, he believed "it to be the supreme duty of American intelligence to devise ways and means for using
most of our 'surpluses' at home." In this and a number
of other ways it was the Beard of the 1930's who spoke
most directly to the New Left. In adopting and updating
these themes New Left historians brought Charles Beard
very much back to the center of the historical stage,
a position, one suspected, he would have found im-
mensely gratifying.[17]

Among the New Left's nonliving heroes Marx seemed
to have received the second greatest amount of respect,
but it is necessary to exercise due caution in apportion-
ing his influence. New revisionists, on the whole, never
adhered to a strict historical materialist interpretation
of social life, nor was their vocabulary that of fellow
travelers. Even those who clearly patterned their approach on the Marxist-Leninist model sought to square
their analyses with peculiar American conditions, the
results of which often appeared labored if not absurd.
The Marxism of the New Left, with few exceptions, was
at bottom a pervasive Marxism which said little about
class conflict and almost nothing about the dictatorship
of the proletariat.

2. WILLIAM APPLEMAN WILLIAMS, AMERICAN DIPLOMACY, AND THE NEW LEFT

The Making of a New Revisionism

Turning to living heroes, William Appleman Williams seemed to have largely influenced the bulk of the New Left diplomatic literature that began to appear in the 1960's. Viewed by the majority of the historical academy as an earnest dissenter, disparaged sometimes bitterly by his critics and previously harassed by such groups as the House Un-American Activities Committee, Williams served as a model and as a source of strength to exponents of the new revisionism writing in the field of American diplomatic history. That Williams's work had a seminal influence on the New Left can hardly be open to question; all that is open to question is the extent to which the new revisionist followed the master.

Leader of the so-called "Wisconsin School of Diplomatic History," Williams laid the groundwork for a small but increasingly influential number of historians who, like himself, conceived a critique of United States external relations as one vehicle in urging, hopefully, the nonviolent replacement of America's presumably expansionist political economy with a democratic socialism that was economically self-sufficient and politically free from international entanglements. At this time it might prove useful to analyze ideas and basic pre–suppositions contained in Williams's published works, paying particular attention to his diplomatic histories, and in so doing raise the following questions: What was there about Williams's formative years to suggest the cause of his dissenting opinions, assuming, as the writer does, that there is a significant connection between an historian's background, training and personality variables on the one hand and the writing of history on the other? What were the nature and substance of his critique of United States foreign policy? To what extent did they indicate the necessity of restructuring American national life? And, finally, what was Williams's legacy to the New Left?

William Appleman Williams was born in Atlantic, Iowa, in 1921. Growing up in a predominantly agricultural setting, Williams developed an understanding of, among other things, farmers and their problems. Although not of farming parents, he had "learned a considerable amount about the history and life of the farmer, and about his relationship with the rest of society, long before I had the slightest intention of being a historian." What seemed to have most impressed him was the often precarious and helpless position of the farmer in a free market economy, the classic grievance of American agrarian radicalism from the Populists to Milo Reno's Farmers' Holiday Association. "Anyone who grew up in Iowa during the Depression," wrote Williams, "learned quickly (and well) about the deep and direct relationship between the fluctuation of the business cycle and the condition of life for the farmer." One could readily

imagine, moreover, that Williams imbibed the agricultural community's traditional noninterventionist outlook, which almost always has viewed the wisdom of
political overseas entanglements with considerable suspicion. It was not until 1969 that Williams himself thoroughly investigated the farmers' role in the formulation
of late nineteenth-century foreign policy, but there could
be little doubt that his initial encounter with a period-
ically downtrodden and historically inward-looking
segment of the population ultimately influenced his resolve to call into question not only the conduct of
American diplomacy but also the nature of American
society.[18]

Despite the tragic loss of his father, who was killed
flying in Army Air Corps maneuvers in 1928, Williams
experienced a normal childhood. What was particularly
striking, however, was the intellectual stimulation he received at an early age, being actively encouraged to read
and to recognize the character and elements of society.
Until he entered the University of Wisconsin Graduate
School in the late 1940's, Williams's formal education
consisted essentially of the military-oriented training he
received at Kemper Military School and the United
States Naval Academy at Annapolis, from which he
received a B.S. in 1944. Williams felt he obtained an
excellent and well-rounded education in both the sci-
ences and the humanities at the Naval Academy, in itself
a remarkable commentary on the alleged rigidity of the
military establishment's educational processes. More
importantly, Williams learned about power and his responsibility for his fellow men, about accepting the consequences of his own actions, and about the individual's
role in the community in which meeting one's obligations
to others was at least as important as exercising his own
will in his own way. At the Naval Academy he also

learned about war, which he considered mankind's worst pedagogy despite its limited and horrible effectiveness. For a man of Williams's sensitivity, a tour of duty as an executive officer in the Pacific Theater of Operations must have given these thoughts special meaning. In sum, by 1945 Williams had acquired what he considered to be a clearly understood system of values and an inquisitive and trained intellect that had a sense of the ironic, the paradoxical and the tragic; most important, he had obtained a knowledge of how the world worked and a sense that it needed to function better.

During the period from 1945 to 1946, like many of the more politically minded members of the New Left Williams sought to make that world function better. In that year he actively participated in the civil rights movement in the South, experiencing intense and close collaboration with blacks in their attempt to improve their lives. In 1946 a spinal injury sustained in the war recurred, necessitating a thirteen-month stay in a number of naval hospitals. During his convalescence Williams contemplated at various times becoming an architect, a novelist or an historian. He decided to become an historian because most of all he wanted to know why. A student of Fred Harvey Harrington, Williams subsequently was graduated with an M.A. and Ph.D. in history from the University of Wisconsin in 1948 and 1950.

From this sketch of Williams's early years it is obvious that no single factor could or should explain his development into a revisionist historiographer; one could suggest only that the cumulative impact contributed to that development. Thus, downtrodden farmers and their discontent with the vicissitudes of a free marketplace economy, their noninterventionist tendencies and their class and anti-big-business consciousness, along with his military training and reaction to it, his view of war at first-hand

and an acute awareness of racial inequality and an effort to do something about it, contributed to the world outlook of William Appleman Williams. Each new encounter gave him knowledge of how the world worked and a growing sense that it needed to function better. This is not to say, however, that the majority of dissenting writers of foreign policy had traveled similar roads or that they had shared comparable education and life experiences. What Williams and the newer revisionists do share equally, one suspects, is their intense and deep dissatisfaction with the workings of American society as it is currently constructed and, as a corollary, its external thrusts. Unlike the intellectuals who are alienated and have gone to mountain communes to make their peace, the new revisionist has opted to stay within the system, making his voice heard, and to do everything this side of violence to effect change.

In addition to having his own value system, Williams approached the study of history with a methodology and a vocabulary that tended to make historical dialogue with those who did not share his views difficult if not impossible. At the outset, Williams's philosophy of history set him apart from the overwhelming majority of historians of his own generation who dominated the historical profession in the postwar period. "History's great tradition," declared Williams in a manner echoing Beard, "is to help us understand ourselves and our world so that each of us, individually and in conjunction with our fellow men, can formulate relevant and reasoned alternatives and become meaningful actors in making history." In short, history must serve current needs. Every historian, to be sure, hopes his research will enlighten the reader, make him better informed, and thus more or less indirectly guide him to make more intelligent decisions concerning the world around him. The

difference in Williams's approach was the sense of im-
mediacy he imported. His messages were urgent and
often apocalyptic, which placed Williams in the van-
guard of C. Vann Woodward's call in the early 1960's
for the return of an apocalyptic historiography. For
example, in an article examining the relationship between Turner's frontier thesis and the drift of twentieth-
century United States foreign policy, about which more
will be said, Williams flatly warned Americans that
unless their thinking changed, they undoubtedly would
share destruction with the rest of mankind. In his words,
"The frontier was now on the rim of hell, and the inferno
was radioactive." He similarly remarked within the context of discussing possible repetition of the Cuban mis-
sile crisis of 1962: "The next Cuba may very well be
the last," the prelude to "the final catastrophe," the form
of which will be "a global fire." This was more than
colorful language; this was the language of finality. In
any case, Williams's apocalyptic vision together with
his philosophy of history seemed to have been passed
on to his followers, and it was just such an approach
that made him so enormously stimulating to younger
New Left historians of the 1960's.[19]

Williams's methodology also served to set him apart
from his contemporaries. The basic tool he used to cut
into what he believed to be the reality of the past was
"the concept of *Weltanschauung,* or definition of the
world and how it works," which taken by itself was not
particularly innovative. Nonetheless, the *Weltanschauung*
concept was crucial to an understanding of Williams,
not only because it amplified his own theory of causation but also, and perhaps more significantly, because
it indicated his total rejection of the psychology-of-
action theory that had permeated much of the postwar
diplomatic literature. Doubtful that it ever was, in

Richard Hofstadter's words, "a psychological common-
place . . . to respond to frustration with acts of aggression, and to allay anxieties by threatening acts against
others," Williams suggested that the individual's *Weltanschauung* worked in a more decidedly rational manner.
He went on to explain that historians who rely overly
upon the psychology of the irrational to explain human
behavior "seem to have confused consciousness of purpose with conspiracy." Having said that, Williams turned
to what he imagined to be the operative American concept of the world.[20]

The *Weltanschauung* of the great majority of Americans throughout their history, according to Williams,
consisted of "having defined everything good in terms
of a surplus of property [a belief which originally derived from an earlier abundance of, and relatively easy
access to, Western lands], the problem . . . [being] one
of developing techniques for securing good things from
a succession of new frontiers." From the beginning of
the Republic the seemingly limitless frontier generally
was regarded as the principal source of national strength,
in that Americans believed "representative government,
economic prosperity, and personal happiness . . . depend[ed] on expansion westward." This view of the
world, however, contained seeds of its own weakness
and, perhaps ultimately, its own destruction. In regarding the expansion of the frontier as a necessary function
and absolute prerequisite both of democracy and capitalism, Americans came to judge "a surplus of property
as a substitute for thought about society." The pursuit
of such an illusion resulted in the "Great Evasion."
Williams contended that above all else, "Frederick Jack-
son Turner understood that his countrymen defined
Nature as the frontier and viewed the frontier as a 'gate
of escape from the bondage of the past.' " Furthermore,

continued Williams, "This has been true, not only in the obvious sense of conquering and managing (and often wasting) the resources of a continent . . . but also in the more fundamental sense of evading the demands of living closely and responsively and creatively with other human beings." With the settlement of the American West in its last stage and the emergence of a highly productive machine society in the last quarter of the nineteenth century, the concept of the necessity of an ever-expanding territorial frontier gradually was replaced by the concept of the necessity of an ever-expanding foreign market, a shift from an agrarian to an industrial imperialism. Immediate consequences of this rationale were war with Spain and establishment of an incipient "informal empire," a commercial empire based on free trade in an open door world. With this as its ultimate objective, American foreign policy found itself "locked" in place for at least the first half of the twentieth century. "Given this expansionist theory of prosperity and history," wrote Williams, "the activities of foreign nations were interpreted almost wholly as events which denied the United States the opportunity for its vital expansion." He noted that "a different explanation of the nation's difficulties would have produced a different estimate of foreign actions, for not one of the countries actually threatened the United States." Thus any nation or system—whether it be imperial or Nazi Germany, Romanov or Stalinist Russia—that sought to carve out exclusive spheres of interest became, by American policy makers' definition of the true, the good and the beautiful, the aggressor. According to Williams, so long as Americans continue to think and act this way, they will never come to grips with reality, never blame themselves for inherent instabilities of a capitalist economy. Even worse, they run the risk of losing their great opportunity to create a truly Christian community, devoid of strife, fear and inequality. For these reasons Williams incessantly and earnestly preoccupied himself with arresting the frontier-expansionist development in the last quarter of the twentieth century. "Unless it is shortly modified and ultimately reversed," he concluded, "the subtle process which shifted the image of the frontier from the continent to an overseas economic empire will transfer it once again, this time to space itself, and the evasion will become literally projected to infinity."[21]

Despite the obvious importance he assigned to economic factors in his frontier-expansionist theory of causation, Williams nonetheless regarded himself as a multi-causational historian, almost never failing to point out the contributory role that America's sense of mission had played in the country's foreign policy. Williams suggested in the context of a discussion concerning the provenance of war that there was no proof whatever that the United States ever entered upon war for the sole purpose of making money. But in another context, and in words that clearly suggested the opposite view, he held that *"American capitalism has never since 1861 functioned effectively enough to decrease economic misery over any significant period of time, save as it has been stimulated by war or cold war."* How did he reconcile the one with the other? "Certain freedoms and liberties," observed Williams, "are essential to capitalists and capitalism, even though capitalists and capitalism are not essential to freedom and liberty. There is no discrepancy, therefore, in going to war to defend, secure, and even extend the particular freedoms and liberties associated with such a market-place political economy." Williams held that the issue was not whether capitalism was a unique cause of war, for it was not, and he maintained that the causes of war plague and operate within every other system of political economy. Yet it did seem demonstrable to him "that capitalism heightens and intensifies the role and impact of economic forces in causing wars." In blurring the distinction between "going to war for a free market place and going to war to defend, secure, and even extend the particular freedoms and liberties associated with such a market-place political economy," Williams set out to construct a fully comprehensive interpretation of American diplomatic history that moved well beyond the Realist critique of his own generation, questioning motives as well as behavior.[22]

Williams argued in effect that, in light of America's traditional world outlook, official foreign policy rhetoric reflected not the simple-minded moralisms of a McKinley, Wilson or Roosevelt, as argued by practitioners of Realism, but rather what was generally perceived to be characteristic attributes of a free enterprise system which casually identified certain democratic institutions and practices with expanding trade in a global open door world. In this manner the allegedly "legalistic-moralistic" language of twentieth-century policy makers became, in a metaphorical sense, only the visible side of the American iceberg. The Realist critique was sound so far as it went, but it never went far enough, failing to plumb the actual source of United States foreign policy conduct. The Realists' assault upon what Williams himself called "the imperialism of idealism" proved useful in explaining such excessive moralistic aspects of the American diplomatic experience as the language of the Truman Doctrine, with its implied overcommitment to free peoples everywhere resisting internal or external aggression. Had they gone further, the Williams thesis implied, the Realists might have discovered to what extent past policy makers' "legalistic-moralistic approach to international problems" embodied an integrity of purpose and, trag-ically for the nation, the true national interest. Finally, they would have seen that given the American mind-set only radical alteration of the political economy could preclude further and inevitable diplomatic failures in this century. Williams, much like Beard before him, con-cluded that there was nothing sacred about America's institutions, nothing inevitable about the way in which the nation's history must unfold, and that it was not yet too late to do something about it.

The theme of American-Russian relations dominated Williams's historical writing in the early 1950's. Unlike such later revisionists as Gabriel Kolko, whose historiog-raphy progressed from a critique of American domes-tic policy, Williams's historiography progressed from a critique of American foreign to domestic policy, the allegedly reactionary nature of America's capitalistic political economy being the point at which they touched. "The historians who came to professional maturity dur-ing and after World War II," wrote Williams of his own development, "were inclined to be concerned with ques-tions involving wars, postwar eras, and the crises con-nected with the cold war. . . . That was certainly my own orientation, and it prompted me to undertake a study of American policy toward the Bolshevik Revolution and the Soviet Union. I was operating on an avowed argu-ment that the study of history was relevant to our own time." The product of that effort, an outgrowth of his dissertation at the University of Wisconsin, was *Amer-ican-Russian Relations, 1781-1947* (1952).[23]

The study's point of departure, despite its somewhat misleading title, was the American purchase of Alaska in 1867, the significance of which indicated a watershed in American-Russian relations. "For the United States," wrote Williams, "it marked the final advance on the continent prior to large-scale efforts to gain an Asiatic outlet in the Pacific." This development combined with Russian expansionism in the same direction placed Russia and America on an unnecessary and, for Williams, unfortunate collision course. In his search for responsibility, which is the hallmark of revisionism, both new and old, Williams found "the financial and industrial powers of the United States [who] came to dominate their domestic market and looked ahead for new opportunities" mostly at fault. For "that movement—the overseas expansion of American economic forces—ultimately clashed with Russian activity along the Amur; and though their respective interests might conceivably have been fruitfully harmonized, the the final result was bitter antagonism."

In consequence, Williams concluded, America's "least serious competitor in the market of either China or Manchuria . . . was nevertheless designated the principal enemy," despite the fact that Russia had "before 1903, helped serve American interests by checking Japanese expansion." Williams's judgment, which tended to overlook the Russian threat to close the door precisely where the United States had most of its trade interests, North China and Manchuria, remained an article of faith among Williams's followers throughout the 1960's. The supposed requirements of the American economy, whose leaders remained ever apprehensive of the domestic implication of an industrial glut, forced America into what should have been rightfully considered a Russian sphere of interest. What could have been done differently? At most, the United States could have restructured itself so that it would no longer be necessary to look outward for markets and investment opportunities; at least, it could have acquiesced in Russian hegemony of an area of Asia in which this nation had no vital interests. As one of Williams's most faithful students put it: "Heresy of heresies, one could abstain from . . . preserving the open door, accept the likelihood of Russian domination of northeast Asia (Siberia, Manchuria, northern China, and perhaps Korea); and then seek to profit from it by establishing—short of overt alliance—intimate economic and diplomatic relations with that country." In any case, the diplomatic atmosphere between the two powers had been poisoned long before the outbreak of Bolshevik Revolution, the pivotal event in modern American-Russian relations.[24]

The key to understanding mid-twentieth-century American-Soviet diplomacy, according to Williams's model of United States foreign policy behavior, lay in the initial response of the country's leaders to the Bolshevik Revolution. It was a fact of the first order that from the beginning Washington's reaction to Lenin's seizure of power was characterized by an admixture of hostility and unreality. Despite hopes to the contrary, wrote Williams, "the policy ultimately formulated was based in part on the assumption that Lenin would miraculously disappear and that the Soviet Government would—because it should—collapse." Who was responsible for this policy, which had for all practical purposes ruled out the possibility of Soviet-American cooperation until events over which they had no control brought them together in 1941, American recognition in 1933 being little more than a probe for markets? Williams held that more than anyone else Secretary of State Robert Lansing and President Woodrow Wilson must assume the burden of guilt. Blinded to "the Bolshevik Government because of its class origin and structure," wrote Williams, "the only course, the Secretary confided to his diary, was to act on the hypothesis that Russia will go 'from bad to worse . . . prepare for the time when Russia will no longer be a military factor in the war,' and sit back 'until some dominant personality arises to end it all.' "[41] From Lansing, asserted Williams, no other course could have been expected. President Wilson followed Lansing's lead; unlike Lansing, he should have known better. "The essential tragedy of Wilson's failure," Williams contended, "lies in the fact that he realized and acknowledged that the Soviets represented a desperate attempt on the part of the dispossessed to share the bounty of industrial civilization." More than anyone else, Wilson "knew that they must be given access to that share if further resort to violence was to be forestalled." Nonetheless, Wilson's "keen insight was first dimmed then ultimately beclouded by antagonism to the Soviets and the conscious desire to expand American influence abroad." In the end, wrote Williams of the President's decision to cooperate with the Allied intervention in Russia, the purpose of which was presumably to overthrow the Bolsheviki, Wilson's desire to expand American influence in China, Manchuria and Siberia outweighed his concern for the Russian people.

Equally important, the argument ran, was Wilson's personal inability, which all too often was America's inability, to restrain himself from interfering in the lives of other people. "Wilson was a great man," Williams quoted Raymond Robins as having said in a related context, "but he had one basic fault. He was willing to do anything for people except to get off their backs and let them live their own lives. He would never let go until they forced him to and then it was too late." Wilson consequently proved to be his own worst enemy. What should Wilson have done? Williams indicated that the proper course would have been to follow the lead of Robins, then American Red Cross observer in Russia, who in his efforts to secure both recognition of and relief for Lenin's government sought to keep alive the Eastern Front while laying the groundwork for expanded

American-Soviet economic relations, which hopefully would provide the basis for future relations.[25]

In his condemnation of American hostility toward the new revolutionary government of Russia, Williams himself overlooked the clearly hostile nature of the Bolshevik regime and its ideology. How did one deal with a movement that sought to export revolution? How was a thoroughly middle-class nation supposed to relate to a government that despised the middle class? As Dexter Perkins more realistically pointed out, "The business classes could hardly fail to view with intense repugnance a system of economic organization which regards them as superfluous, as exploiters, as the source and root of all economic evil." Moreover, it was surely open to doubt that the Bolsheviki comprised a *de facto* government in 1917 to 1919, i.e., traditional and common sense diplomatic practices might well have precluded recognition in this period, however enlightened the United States Government. At any rate, to deny that American doubts concerning the acceptability of the Bolshveki regime rested on legitimate ground was to underestimate what is perhaps the single most important component of foreign-policy formulation, the human element or what has at times been called the human nature of foreign policy. The United States response to Bolshevism, given the situational context in which it took place in contrast to the action-reaction mechanism of predetermined open door policy requirements of a capitalist political economy, was logical and, in a strict diplomatic sense, correct. Rather than being blinded by the glare of Bolshevism's societal reordering, American policy makers, and this was especially true of Secretary of State Robert Lansing, had a reasonably accurate understanding of what was taking place in Lenin's Russia.[26]

From a somewhat different perspective, Williams's analysis of the official United States reaction to the Russian Revolution clearly revealed both the function of New Left diplomatic historiography, which sought to call into question the nature of American society by a critique of its external relations, and the inner workings of the author's mind. If it could be demonstrated "that the Soviets represented a desperate attempt on the part of the dispossessed to share the bounty of industrial civilization," then perhaps it also could be demonstrated that Washington's opposition to that goal was symptomatic of a political economy that similarly denied the realization of a better life to the dispossessed of America. Under these circumstances the failure of American diplomacy could become the failure of American society, the lesson being that until the latter was corrected the former would have little chance of succeeding. In this sense a critique of foreign relations became the back door to reform.

Williams attempted to explain subsequent American-Soviet relations in the light of capitalist hostility to the Soviets, citing United States intervention in Russia, the continued policy of nonrecognition in the 1920's, and the policy of noncooperation in the 1930's despite the increasing threat of Hitlerian Germany to world peace. "The theme of American-Russian relations from 1940 to 1947 was a slow modification of the antagonism and indifference of the late 1930's in the direction of accommodation, the breakdown of these efforts, and the substitution . . . of the policy of containment," Williams declared. Although no friend of Soviet Russia, he evidenced little doubt that the Soviets were prepared to cooperate with the United States in the postwar world soon to be created. The Kremlin's leaders wanted only guarantees of strategic security in Eastern Europe and the wherewithal for economic rehabilitation of war-torn areas, neither of which seemed excessive, in view of traditional

Russian fears and the extent to which the Red Army had carried the war against Nazi Germany. Who or what prevented this cooperation? Franklin Roosevelt's repeated insistence upon a policy of postponement, asserted Williams, needlessly fed the fears of the already suspicious Russians who were seeking to implement their own idea of security. In point of fact, wrote Williams, "These objectives were neither denied nor disguised by the Soviets, but the United States failed to formulate a policy in response until the opportunity to negotiate a firm understanding on both issues had been lost." But, as Williams himself suggested, historical reality seldom, if ever, admits of a simple explanation. There was, according to Williams, no easy answer to the question of who started the Cold War, and it would have been highly unhistorical to look for one. The deterioration of American-Soviet relations, he reasoned in a manner resembling Realist analysis, evolved in a complex fashion. In *American Russian Relations* he delineated three stages of the Cold War. "First," he argued, "came the wartime refusal to reach territorial settlement on the basis of Russia's 1941 proposals *before* the Red Army carried the frontier farther West. Then once that opportunity had been lost—the failure to link resolution of the new problem with Russia's postwar economic needs . . . [And finally] in Asia, where the basic territorial commitments were made, the subsequent failure to validate them by facing the challenge of the Bolshevik Revolution in terms of China's *internal* development." Williams was not surprised to find Truman and his advisors unwilling to recognize the attempt on the part of the Chinese Communists "to share the bounty of industrial civilization," their opposition bearing a marked similarity to the manner in which Wilson had previously responded to the Bolsheviks of Russia.[27]

"There remained, under the circumstances," continued

Williams, "but one way to secure Allied solidarity once Germany and Japan were defeated: use Russia's preoccupation with economic rehabilitation as the means to secure negotiated settlements. When this approach was abandoned—or, more exactly, ignored—the Cold War was declared by default. For without negotiation the highly prized freedom of action could be achieved only by force, a fact that was to be formalized in George Kennan's policy of containment." By adopting the containment policy, whose unequivocal objective was either the alteration or destruction of the Soviet system of government, the Truman Administration, in Williams's view, unilaterally abandoned whatever chance there was of a negotiated settlement and must for this reason alone assume a large measure of responsibility for the coming of the Cold War and a generation of misunderstanding. In short, American diplomacy announced to the world that it was bankrupt.[28]

In 1969 Williams reflected that during the seven years following the publication of *American-Russian Relations* (1952) he had become increasingly persuaded of how short a period of time comprised his context. Several ideas began to emerge and take form during those seven years. "The powerful minds of teachers like Fred Harvey Harrington and Paul Farmer, and the confrontation with human reality that comes from sustained research in primary-source materials," wrote Williams, "quickly disabused me of the idea that American-Russian relations could be understood in terms of the thirty years between 1917 and 1947." He consequently extended his research in an attempt to place the Cold War in greater perspective. He began to recognize "that many Americans had thought in terms of, and had acted on, the central thesis of Turner's frontier thesis long before Turner had been born; and they had used such supposedly twentieth-century concepts and phrases as 'the safety valve' in discussing the usefulness or necessity of expansion in solving America's problem." Dealing with American diplomatic history in general and American-Soviet relations in particular, the product of this reappraisal was *The Tragedy of American Diplomacy,* first published in 1959 and revised and enlarged in 1962.[29]

In the *Tragedy of American Diplomacy,* probably his most influential study for the New Left historians, Williams argued that "the tragedy of American Diplomacy is not that it is evil, but that it denies and subverts American ideas and ideals. The result is a most realistic failure, as well as an ideological and moral one; for in being unable to make the American system function satisfactorily without recourse to open door expansion (and by no means perfectly even then), American diplomacy suffers by comparison with its own claims and ideas as well as other approaches." The engine powering this drive was the American *Weltanschauung* that the nation's "freedom and prosperity depended upon the continued expansion of its economic and ideological system through the policy of the open door." Within this framework Williams went on to analyze the Spanish-American War, the open door notes, United States entry both into World War I and World War II, and the Cold War.[30]

Turning first to the Spanish-American War, Williams contended that "if there is any one key to understanding the coming of the war with Spain, it very probably lies in the growing conviction among top economic and political leaders that American military intervention was necessary in order to clean up the Cuban mess so that domestic *and other foreign policy* issues could be dealt with efficiently and effectively," a theme fully explored by Williams's followers. Williams suggested that such other factors as the jingoistic press and aroused nationalism were not unimportant, although he had little patience with historians who sought out conspiratorial explanations. Although doubtless true that men occasionally have acted for purely monetary reasons, he maintained that American policy makers on the whole operated within a broader, more conscious frame of reference. Specifically, wrote Williams to the point, "men like McKinley and other national leaders thought about American problems and welfare in an inclusive systematized way that *emphasized* economics . . . wanting democracy and social peace, they argued that economic depression threatened those objectives, and concluded that overseas economic expansion provided a primary means of ending that danger." From this level of analysis, continued Williams, they pursued neither war nor profit for its own sake. In the end, "Their own conception of the world ultimately led them into war in order to solve the problems in the way they considered necessary and best." Ten years later Williams altered this interpretation: "The primary force producing the war against Spain was the market place-expanionist outlook generated by the agricultural majority of the country during the generation in the firing on Fort Sumter. That social consciousness involved an image of the world as a free market place in which personal and social freedoms were casually integrated with economic liberty, in which ideas and experience were merged as beliefs, and which promised ideal results from necessary actions." Pulling the agricultural businessmen along, the thesis ran, the metropolitans "explicitly formulated the war against Spain over Cuba as a war for the free market place in the Far East." Within this context McKinley, as leader of the industrial wing of the Republican Party, sought not only to gain control of the party at home but also to seize a springboard to the Orient. "McKinley," wrote Williams, "was unquestionably prepared to go to war, and to fight the war with a two-front strategy, whenever he judged the agricultural militants on the verge of splitting and taking control of the Republican party, and thereby displacing the metropolis as the dominant force in the political economy." In this sense, then, suggested Williams, "It was one of the most striking displays of presidential nerve and finesse in the nation's history."[31]

Williams's analysis of the origins and consequences of the Spanish-American War in *The Tragedy of American Diplomacy* assumed a position of crucial importance in his historiography, in that he tended to draw a straight line from the developments of 1898 to those of 1970. With corporate capital securely in the driver's seat, the war served as a prelude to the annunciation of the Hay open door notes, which in turn marked the formal announcement of America's bid for an economic empire. As Williams noted in a related but different context, "American policy makers designed their imperial strategy with a view to creating and maintaining the conditions which would enable their nation's power to produce the desired economic and political victories." Inasmuch as "They viewed war as the great disruptor of economic progress, and as the nightrider of political and social regression, their broad objective was to establish rules of the game which would prevent the struggle in the market place from becoming a trial by arms." The word "empire," as used by Williams, should not be understood in the traditional seventeenth or nineteenth-century sense of colonialism. "When an advanced industrial nation plays, or tries to play, a controlling and one-sided role in the development of a weaker economy," he declared, "then the policy of the more powerful country can with accuracy and candor only be described as imperial." Moreover, "The empire that results may well be informal in the sense that the weaker country is not ruled on a day-to-day basis by resident administrators, or increasingly populated by emigrants from the advanced country, but it is nevertheless an empire." Thus twentieth-century American diplomatic history became, for Williams, a story of the struggle for empire, albeit an informal one.[32]

On the basis of Williams's lexicon of diplomatic terms one was given to understand with regard to United States entry into World War I that "whatever the faults and sins of England and France, they were better than autocratic Germany. [For] America could work with them toward a peaceful, prosperous, and moral world, whereas such would be impossible if Germany won." Or one might read of United States entry into World War II: "The pattern of American expansion under the principles and procedures of the open door notes came to maturity during the 1920's. And it was the threat posed to that program by the combined impact of the Great Depression and the competing expansion of Germany and Japan . . . which ultimately accounted for American entry into World War II." This is not to say that Williams dismissed such other factors as ideological affinity with the Western powers; what he did, however, was subordinate them to a secondary position.[33]

Having done so, Williams set out to modify and elaborate his previous assessment of the origins of the Cold War. Upon the death of President Roosevelt, who had showed little promise of reconciling the open door strategy with the changed postwar world, Williams said that "the great majority [of American policy makers] rapidly embarked upon a program to force the Soviet Union to accept America's traditional conception of itself and the world. This decision represented the final stage in the transformation of the policy of the open door from a utopian idea into an ideology, from an intellectual out-

look for a changing world into one concerned with preserving it in the traditional mold." In this manner,
continued Williams, "The philosophy and practice of
open door expansion had become in both its missionary
and economic aspects *the* view of the world," a conclusion shared by a number of clearly non-New Left historians who do not subscribe to Williams's frontier-
expansionist theory of causation and all that it implies.

At any rate, the Soviets were offered no choice, particularly with the addition of the atomic bomb to the
American arsenal of military and economic weapons. At
this point Williams entered into a most curious discussion
of Cold War responsibility.[34] To say that the United
States gave the Soviets no choice, began Williams, "is not
to say that the United States started or caused the Cold
War," because in a larger sense it was the rise and fall of
Hitlerian Germany that brought "the United States and
the Soviet Union . . . into direct and sustained confrontation from the Baltic to the Black Sea." He continued, "The real issue . . . is not which side started the
Cold War," but "rather the far more subtle one of which
side committed its power to policies which hardened the
natural and inherent tensions and propensities into bitter
antagonisms and inflexible positions." Although neither
side was free from blame or in any sense "innocent"—
the Russian decision to extend communism on the bay-
onet of the Red Army perhaps being "the real tragedy of
Soviet diplomacy"—two facts, according to Williams,
were uncontestable: first, *"The United States had from
1944 to at least 1962 a vast preponderance of actual as
well as potential power vis-a-vis the Soviet Union";*
second, "The United States used or deployed its preponderance of power wholly within the assumption and
the tradition of the open door policy." In the final
analysis, ended Williams, "The United States never

formulated and offered the Soviet Union a settlement based on other, less grandiose, terms." The failure to reach a *modus vivendi* with the Soviets as the war drew to a close constituted, for Williams, the great *Tragedy of American Diplomacy* in the twentieth century.[35]

If his discussion of Cold War responsibility appeared somewhat opaque and vulnerable to criticism of world juggling, which is undeniably true, there could be no question concerning his essay's concluding message. America, and here Williams spoke most directly to the younger generation of New Left historians, must put its own house in order before turning to the outside world. Americans had to recognize that the last frontier was not to be found in Asia, Africa or outer space but at home. The task was one of restructuring their capitalist political economy along democratic socialist lines, to create a society free and self-sufficient. Americans also had to recognize, finally, that the nation's political and economic well-being rested neither on global open door expansion nor on forcing its own beliefs and institutions on rising peoples everywhere, but rather on what Williams called "the rational and equitable use of its own human and material resources at home and in interdependent cooperation with all other peoples of the world." In this manner, argued Williams, United States foreign policy would be geared toward helping other nations realize their own goals on their own. "The essence of such a policy," he wrote, "would be an open door for revolutions." Then, and only then, he concluded in a tone reminiscent of Beard's hopeful expectation twenty-five years ago, "having come to terms with themselves—having achieved maturity—Americans could exhibit the self-discipline necessary to let other peoples come to terms with themselves."[36]

Williams's *The United States, Cuba, and Castro* added

little more either to the author's methodology or inter-pretation. American policy makers again, as in the case of Bolshevik Russia and Communist China, allegedly were blinded by the fact that Castro and his followers "represented a desperate attempt on the part of the dis-possessed to share the bounty of industrial civilization," for "it is essential to realize that Cuba was a society of disparate contrasts and staggering contradictions strug-gling to break finally free of the limitations of an un-balanced and lurching economy," Williams averred. When the United States could have helped most, it helped least, "quickly [and wrongly] interpret [ing] Castro's action of late 1959, and his trade deal with the Soviet Union early in 1960, as meaning that Cuba had become a totalitarian Communist satellite." So far as historiog-raphy was concerned, Williams's principal contribution in this study was his extended treatment of what he be-lieved was an American tendency to externalize good as well as evil.[37]

"The American propensity to externalize evil," argued Williams, "is at least as well developed as any known to history. We have followed that self-righteous path of least resistance since we won our independence." Having said that, however, he declared, "What is not so generally recog-nized, however, is the degree to which Americans have also externalized good. The extent, that is, to which they have argued (and finally assumed) that America's politi-cal and economic well-being are determined by oppor-tunities that exist outside the United States." By implying that the American political economy hardly could be expected to reconcile its world outlook with a people's revolution in Cuba, Williams again called for the recon-struction of American society through a critique of its external relations. What most bothered Williams was that the American-supported invasion of Cuba was a natural (and inevitable) reflex action on the part of the nation's leaders. If America had, however, a different perspective, a perspective which focused inward instead of outward, it would have been difficult to imagine a response of this nature. In the end, contended Williams, "We in America have judged Castro as though the United States moved from the conditions of 1776 to those of 1962 through a process of joyful good will and immaculate rationality. The point of this lesson about revolutions is that the truly moral and intelligent objectives for outsiders involve help to reduce those costs [of modernization] to the lowest possible level—not demands that the revolution be abandoned, or sermons about evil men who refuse to give up their mistaken goals."[38]

In summary, a critical analysis of the ideas and basic presuppositions contained in Williams's published studies suggest that his principal contribution to the New Left diplomatic literature that emerged in the 1960's was the general thesis, in his words, that "empire is as American as apple pie." Through his frontier-expansionistic theory of causation, which assumed that United States foreign policy derived rationally and logically (if routinely) from an inherently expansionist capitalist political economy, Williams revived and updated an earlier economic revisionism, subsumed and moved beyond the Realist critique of his own generation, and called for the reconstruction of American national life along democratic socialist lines, economically self-sufficient and politically free from overseas entanglements. In so doing, Williams passed on to the new revisionism a basically ironic interpretation of American diplomatic history which attempted to show that as more and more America pursued peace and the expectation of prosperity through the construction of a stable, freely trading open door world, greater and greater became the illusion of long-term prosperity and less and less the chance of peace. A view of foreign policy that sought only to project its own image onto the world flew in the face of history and was doomed from the beginning. Williams passed to the new revisionists a presentist concept of history, a sense of urgency, and, most importantly, an apocalyptic vision of the failure to heed his warning.[39]

3. THE NEW LEFT AND THE RECONSTRUCTION OF UNITED STATES DIPLOMATIC HISTORY, 1898-1941

In Pursuit of an Open Door World

The New Left reconstruction of late nineteenth and early twentieth-century United States diplomatic history that emerged in the decade of the sixties marked the recrudescence of an essentially economic interpretation of American foreign policy. The purpose of the following section is to describe and examine ideas contained in various New Left interpretations of major themes and critical turning points in United States diplomacy during the period approximately from 1898 to 1941: the origin and significance of the Spanish-American War, the debate concerning the annexation of the Philippines, the Hay open door notes, American entry into World War I, the League of Nations, and American involvement in World War II.

Rejecting the interpretation of older, more traditional foreign policy historians who primarily explained the emergence of late nineteenth and early twentieth-century expansion in terms almost exclusively territorial and unintentional, New Left historian Walter LaFeber argued in *The New Empire* (1963) that the external thrust of the United States in the late 1890's was, given the system that generated policy, both logical and intentional. "The overseas empire that America controlled in 1900," wrote LaFeber, "was not a break in history, but a natural culmination." He added, moreover, that the evidence overwhelmingly suggested "Americans neither acquired this empire during a temporary absence of mind nor had the empire forced upon them." LaFeber's overall impression of American policy makers in this period, in contradiction to that of the Realists and other diplomatic historians who have painted a scenario of impractical idealistic and bumbling politicians with little or no understanding of the far-reaching implications of their decisions, "found the policy makers and the businessmen of this era to be responsible, conscientious men who accepted the economic and social realities of their time, understood [the nature of the connection between] domestic and foreign problems, debated issues vigorously, and especially were unafraid to strike out on new and uncharted paths in order to create what they sincerely hoped would be a better nation and a better people." The point of departure for the new empire, according to the revisionist model of United States diplomatic behavior, was the establishment of a highly industrialized machine society in the last half of the nineteenth century. The new empire began to take form about the time that William Seward became Lincoln's Secretary of State, and it differed from its predecessor in two important respects. First, with the completion of the continental conquest Americans moved with increasing authority into such extra-continental areas as Hawaii, Latin America, Asia and Africa; second, the empire's form had altered to the extent that "instead of searching for farming, mineral or grazing lands, Americans sought foreign markets for agricultural staples or industrial goods." More than any other single factor, the completion of this development marked what LaFeber called a major watershed in American history. Any interpretation omitting this fact in explaining United States expansionism at this time, according to LaFeber's analysis, missed the point. The structural requirements of the political economy, whether real or imagined, forced America outward, rather than aroused nationalism brought on by the Spanish-American War or the misguided idealism that allegedly informed a version of America's white man's burden.[40]

Probing the attitude of the American public in general and of the policy makers in particular that accompanied this external outlook, LaFeber indicated that the course taken by United States diplomacy in the 1890's could not be understood fully without first comprehending the precise nature of the relationships between domestic and foreign policy in the period lasting approximately from 1850 to 1889. "Spurred by a fantastic industrial revolution, which produced ever larger quantities of surplus goods, depressions and violence, and warned by a growing radical literature that the system was not functioning properly, the United States prepared to solve its dilemma with foreign expansion," LaFeber asserted. To LaFeber, and here he addressed himself most directly to other new revisionists who similarly regarded their critique of United States external policy as a vehicle with which to urge the reform of America's capitalist political economy, the alternatives were unmistakably clear: "Either radically readjust the political institutions to a nonexpanding society or find new areas of expansion." Having chosen the second alternative, which hardly could have been surprising in a market place economy anchored to middle-class beliefs in free enterprise and private property, the only real differences among the overwhelming majority of American foreign policy leaders from that time onward were over means rather than ends. The goal itself, "expansion in the form of trade instead of landed settlement," never was seriously questioned. LaFeber, like William Appleman Williams before him, contended that the nation's quest for markets necessarily (and unfortunately) meant a realignment of friend and foe alike, and in a real sense predetermined the course of American diplomatic history. To be sure, he noted, some of the reordering resulted from matters outside the dictates of the new empire, such as Jewish pogroms and general repugnance to autocratic government in Russia and Germany. Having said that, however, LaFeber went on to what he considered the heart of the problem: expansionist tendencies structurally inherent in America's political economy. "Clearly," he wrote, "the dynamics of the new empire in Latin America, Samoa, and especially in the Far East played a critical role in this realignment, a realignment that had begun to be evident in the 1890's and increasingly important in the twentieth century." LaFeber's emphasis on this point implied, if his premise were carried to its logical conclusion, that a differently structured political economy would have meant a different course for American diplomacy. And one suspected this was exactly what LaFeber would have preferred.[41]

Turning to the administration of William McKinley and origins of the Spanish-American War, LaFeber pointed out that the President had at least three options before him, any one of which could have brought the Cuban Revolution to an end. First, wrote LaFeber, McKinley "could have let the Spanish forces and the insurgents fight until one or the other fell exhausted from the bloodshed and financial strain"; second, "he could have demanded an armistice and Spanish assurance that negotiations over the summer would result in some solution which would pacify American feelings"; or third, he "could have demanded both an armistice and Spanish assurance that Cuba would become independent immediately," and "if Spain would not grant both of these conditions, American military intervention would result." Why did McKinley take the third option? What did he hope to achieve by it? The President, according to LaFeber's argument, did not want war *per se,* and there could be little reason to doubt that he had actually sought a peaceful solution. "By mid-March, however," declared LaFeber categorically, "he was beginning to discover that, although he did not want war, he did want what only war could provide: the disappearance of the terrible uncertainty in American political and economic life, and a solid basis with which to resume the building of the new commercial empire."

What was the role of yellow journalism and the undisguised warlike mood of the Congress? To be certain, such elements should be treated as crucial, but they must be used with caution. For example, wrote LaFeber, "A first observation should be that Congress and the yellow press, which had been loudly urging intervention since 1895, did not make a maiden appearance in March, 1898." More important, he averred, "was the transformation of the opinion of many spokesmen for the business community who had formerly opposed war." Why was this judgment reached in 1898 and not sooner? Among other reasons, which for some probably included immediate material gain, "was the uncertainty that plagued the business community in mid-March"; for it became increasingly apparent that "such an unpredictable economic basis could not provide the springboard for the type of overseas commercial empire that Mc-Kinley and numerous businessmen envisioned." In short, capitalists and capitalism abhor uncertainty. At this point LaFeber made it unequivocally clear that, although it was doubtless true war with Spain would provide businessmen with an opportunity for furthering their own economic expansion, the war itself did not provide the impetus for that expansion. Instead, the road to war, in LaFerber's judgment, had "been provided by the impact of the industrial revolution, especially the depression that followed the panic of 1893."[42]

LaFeber next turned his attention to the imperial debate that attended the aftermath of the war. The earlier acquisitions of Alaska, the Midway Islands and Pago Pago in Samoa were connected with the acquisitions of Hawaii and the Philippines in that "the United States obtained these areas not to fulfill a colonial policy, but to use their holdings as a means to acquire markets for the glut of goods pouring out of highly mechanized factories and farms." In this light, continued LaFeber, policy makers regarded these areas "as strategic means to obtaining and protecting objectives which they defined as economic." Given the two basic premises upon which LaFeber conceived his estimate to rest, the control of these areas assumed a logic of its own. In the first place, wrote LaFeber, there was "the general consensus reached by the American business community and policy makers in the 1890's that additional foreign markets would solve the economic, social and political problems created by the industrial revolution"; in the second place, there was "the growing belief that, however great its industrial prowess, the United States needed strategic bases if it hoped to compete successfully with government-supported European enterprises in Asia and Latin

America." On the first premise Americans generally agreed; on the second premise they exhibited important differences. Else how explain the fact that three of the most prominent leaders of the anti-annexationist cause— Walter Gresham, Edward Atkinson and Carl Schurz— were at the same time exponents of expanded free trade? Within this framework, added LaFeber, indicating the bogus character of the debate that followed, "It may be suggested that one fruitful way to approach the 'imperialist versus anti-imperialist' clash in the 1890's is to view the struggle in terms of a narrow and limited debate on the question of which tactical means the nation should use to obtain commonly desired objectives"—an anti-colonial commercial empire." The debate could be rephrased as: on the one hand, averred LaFeber, comparatively "few Americans believed that the Latin American and Asian markets were of little importance to the expansive American industrial complex; on the other hand, few agreed . . . that the United States should claim and occupy every piece of available land in the Pacific." LaFeber's argument is predicated on belief that public opinion assumed a middle ground between these two views and that within that area of consensus the imperial debate took place.[43]

Whatever form the debate assumed, LaFeber had no doubt that America sought and obtained a far-flung commercial empire by the end of the century. The new empire that surfaced showed every sign of having resulted from a conscious design that was prepared carefully by policy makers and leaders who could see little or no alternative. LaFeber argued in essence that, contrary to conventional interpretations that relied heavily on such factors as misguided idealism and lack of design in explaining the emergence of late nineteenth-century United States expansion, the American empire that emerged in these years derived rationally and with clear purpose from a capitalist political economy whose structural requirement demanded foreign markets for an ever-growing surplus of industrial goods and agricultural staples. The so-called "great national aberration" became, in New Left hands, no aberration at all.

In *China Market* (1967) Thomas J. McCormick reinforced and carried through LaFeber's theme of an American commercial empire to the promulgation of the Hay open door notes. McCormick's characterization of his own work "as an economic interpretation—a fact that requires no apologies but does necessitate a few qualifications" sheds considerable light on the general approach that informed much of the new revisionist literature concerning this particular period in United States diplomatic history. McCormick said of his own approach, that under no circumstances should his work be considered "a narrow economic interpretation—a 'pocketbook' determinism—that centers on special interest groups and efforts to shape policy according to their special needs." Moreover, he noted, "This is not to deny that such interplay existed or to say it was unimportant, but simply to suggest that its ultimate impact on policy was more modest than one might usually assume; that, indeed at times, policy formulation proved curiously immune to interests' pressures." This could be explained by the obvious fact that business interests seldom posed a monolithic front as well as by the fact that elements within the business community often worked at cross purposes, offering and supporting policies that best served their own particular needs. "But this also reflects the reality," remarked McCormick, "that policy makers and a great many business leaders as well sometimes operated from a more sophisticated and cosmopolitan position than many functional spokesmen; they were more precisely cognizant of the larger relationships between foreign policy and the ongoing effort to save the status quo from its own stresses and strains." Given this mind-set, "and because they analyzed the causes of social instability as economic," declared McCormick, "their attempts at social rationalization were necessarily economic as well."

McCormick further maintained that the decision-making process lay almost exclusively in the hands of the late nineteenth-century power elite, which he then defined as "those social elements with the most *direct power* to influence national decisions and other events, and/or those who controlled property and affected the social relationships that flowed from that control—in short, the business community (exclusive of small and local enterprises) and its political and intellectual allies." Thus, McCormick sought to demonstrate that the drive behind policy making was a class consciousness rather than function, "a near-consensus, fairly sophisticated class consciousness about the imperative need to rationalize a shaky order." Like LaFeber, McCormick advanced the thesis that such late nineteenth and early twentieth-century American expansionism as Hawaii, the Philippines and especially the open door notes, stemmed from the generally perceived necessity to sustain this shaky social order through a continuously expanding commercial empire, the practical application of which resembled a sort of "free-trade imperialism." McCormick's argument rested squarely on the premise that "the two and a half decades between the Panic of 1873 and the war with Spain encompassed one of the most profound social crises in American history—the inability of laissez-faire capitalism to function either rationally or equitably in a period of rapid industrial maturation." The consequences of such a development were "skyrocketing production which made America an industrial giant second to none" on one hand and, on the other, "plummeting prices, falling rates of profit, and enervating depressions—the crisis of overdevelopment."[44]

The root cause of America's difficulty lay in overproduction, both of an actual and potential nature, which derives from a highly mechanized market-place economy. McCormick conceded, however, that this particular tendency could not be attributed to the economic system *per se*. He pointed out, "The closing of traditional areas of investment, such as railroads and western lands, flooded capital into more narrowly productive channels, while the technological revolution produced more goods per dollar invested." McCormick then added—and here, like LaFeber, he went to the heart of the new revisionism's special pleading—"But to perhaps a greater degree, surplus production reflected an endemic quality of laissez-faire capitalism: overcompetition, wasteful, duplicative, self-destructive competition, which made the industrial order into a dog-eat-dog Social Darwinistic arena"; in the end, the "economy . . . was chaotic, unstable, unplanned, and unpredictable, one that could not resolve its own dilemma." The only real alternative, which comparatively few Americans bothered to consider, was "some equitable change in the pattern of income distribution and effective consumer demand." From a different perspective, concluded McCormick, "The nation's fundamental problem was underconsumption," the implication being of course "that any lasting solution would have to be an internal one." This overproduction analysis, together with the social unrest accompanying it, produced among many Americans, and particularly among the power elite who controlled the levers of government, an underlying agreement that something had to be done to relieve the industrial glut that threatened to overwhelm the system. Consequently, wrote McCormick, "It is clear that the real 'great debate' on expansion ended *before* 'America's Colonial Experiment' began. It centered on the nature of the social and economic crisis, and its resolution defined, as a major component of the national interest, the goal of a new frontier in the market outlets of the world." The imperial debate that followed, as allegedly would be so with all American foreign policy debate throughout the twentieth century, revolved around means rather than ends, focusing on the question "whether or not economic expansion required the accoutrement of a colonial empire for its successful fulfillment; whether closed markets or open doors would be most effective." With these choices before them American policy makers consciously and deliberately opted for the creation of a freely trading open door world based on the principle of equality of commercial opportunity, free from violence and revolution, and committed to democratic institutions and practices: in short, America's capitalist political economy projected onto the world. Thus the open door became, in the New Left model, "a means of avoiding conflict, not creating it; a means of acquiring the economic fruits of empire without *extensive* political-military responsibilities and burdens."[45]

McCormick also held that the American open door approach in China at the turn of the century provided the blueprint for United States diplomacy *vis-a-vis* the underdeveloped nations of the world throughout the twentieth century. McCormick wrote, "In essence the United States defined Chinese integrity in terms of preserving her territory intact, maintaining the external symbols of her sovereignty, and upholding national pride and face—all necessary to give legality and credence to the open door." Upon closer examination, however, "the American definition denied to China either the right or capacity to modify or close the open door, or develop a more balanced, advanced and sophisticated economy." Viewed in this light, concluded McCormick, Hay's treatment of China "was the classic precursor for America's general twentieth-century attitude toward economic development in underdeveloped areas—from the Boxer Rebellion to Harry S. Truman's Four Point Program." Although "Chinese modernization was to be encouraged in—and limited to—agricultural diversification and specialized light industry, heavy industrialization and across-the-board consumer manufacturing were to remain *verboten*."[46]

Where the larger issue of American-Russian relations was concerned, McCormick saw three alternatives open to United States policy makers after the Boxer Rebellion. First, the United States could have continued to pursue "collective acceptance of the open door in the hope that circumstances of other nation's foreign policies might undergo a change for the better." Second, the United States could have acquiesced in what appeared to be the imminent partition of China, taking "a join-them-if-you-cannot-beat-them attitude, carving out as generous a sphere of influence as possible." Third and finally, the United States "could [have] abstain[ed] from either partitioning or preserving the open door, accept[ed] the likelihood of Russian dominance of northeast Asia (Siberia, Manchuria, and perhaps Korea); and then seek to profit from it by establishing—short of overt alliance—intimate economic and diplomatic relations with that country." The last alternative was, for McCormick, the most logical course to have followed: "for by 1901 it was possible to argue that circumstances had changed; that there no longer existed, as there had been in 1898–1900, any real chance of preventing Russian emasculation of the open door; that short of employing force, the thing to do was to face the hard facts of life and make the best of them." It is not coincidental that McCormick's prescription for United States diplomacy at the turn of the century became part and parcel of the New Left prescription for United States diplomacy in the post-1945 period. It was central to his argument that as early as 1900 American foreign policy found itself both "locked" in place and headed on a collision course with Russia by virtue of adherence to an open door policy that presumably violated what rightly should have been considered, by any criteria, a Russian sphere of interest. Rephrased, if it could be demonstrated that the open door policy of the United States was inimical to Russian interests a number of years before the advent of the Bolshevik regime, then it also might be demonstrated that the American decision to pursue such a policy after World War II contributed in no mean way to the coming of the Cold War, assuming of course, as the New Left uniformly does, that Soviet behavior has primarily been motivated by traditional Russian goals and fears, the ideological appearance of international communism to the contrary notwithstanding. Supposedly had America then pursued a different foreign policy, the course of American diplomacy would have been different and, hopefully, better adjusted to the realities of other great nations aspiring to fill their own needs in their own way. Similarly, had America been something other than a capitalist political economy, which, rightly or wrongly, identified the perpetuation of an open-door world with the only real solution to the structural maladjustments that usually attend an overdeveloped industrial society, then it also is conceivable that American foreign policy would have, at the very least, been less imperialistic than it was.[47]

In summary, LaFeber and McCormick jointly contributed to a construction of late nineteenth and early twentieth-century American expansionism that differed markedly from previous orthodox interpretations in terms of emphases. Such factors as Social Darwinism, Manifest Destiny or the perversion of it, "the psychic crisis of the 1890's," and the influence of foreign examples on the nation's foreign policy public all certainly were either discussed or alluded to; but none of these factors was recognized as intelligible considered apart from the increasingly perceived necessity of American policy makers together with the underlying consensus among the majority of the American people to seek a freely trading open-door world for America's ever-growing industrial output and agricultural staples. Unlike conventional historians, the New Left insisted there was nothing particularly innocent or misguided about such a decision, nor was it particularly irrational or unintended. On the contrary, the new revisionism contended that, given the nature of the American political economy, United States foreign policy in this period derived rationally and logically from an inherently expansionistic domestic system that tended to associate both its prosperity and well-being with an ever-expanding frontier of commercial expansion. Rather than restructure the system, by building a more equitable, less wasteful, and, presumably, nonexpansionist society and coming to terms with maladjustment caused by overproduction at home, policy makers opted to export the social problem. Subsequent United States diplomatic history, according to the New Left model, was at best unintelligible considered apart from this development.

The three New Left historians whose historiography in the 1960's concerned itself most directly with the nature of the relationships between Wilsonian diplomacy and American entry into World War I were N. Gordon Levin, Jr., Arno J. Mayer and Carl P. Parrini. In *Wood-*

row Wilson and World Politics (1968), a rather sophisticated analysis that does not de-emphasize the role
of ideals, Levin advanced the proposition that the "ultimate Wilsonian goal may be defined as the attainment
of a peaceful liberal capitalist world under international
law, safe both from traditional imperialism and revolutionary socialism, within whose stable liberal confines a
missionary America could find moral and economic pre-
eminence," i.e., a Wilsonian open door world. Like the
Realist critique which underscored what it imagined to
be the overly "legalistic-moralistic" content of Wilsonian
diplomacy, Levin found that a high degree of moralism
and mission did indeed inform much of Wilson's thinking.

Unlike the Realist critique, however, Levin maintained that Wilson's approach to external affairs was not
at odds with the national interest. "In Wilson's view,"
wrote Levin, "it was America's historic mission to bring
Europe into a peaceful international order based on
world law." More specifically, continued Levin, Wilson
hoped "to create an international civil society, or social
contract, making orderly and responsible world citizens
out of the hitherto aggressive European nations." In this
sense Wilson set out to "Lockeanize" or to Americanize
the international political order under a set of rules, the
whole of which was to be preserved through means of
the moral and material strength of the global social contract found in the League of Nations Charter. Thus the
League of Nations was chosen as the instrument with
which to implement an American-led open door world.
Put yet another way, it was the method chosen "to end
traditional imperialism and the balance of power without socialist revolution, by reforming world politics from
within." In this manner Wilson sought to lay the groundwork for a world order that best would be receptive to
the American perception of its role in the world, its lib-

eral constitutions and practices, and, not accidentally, to a freely trading open door world in which the United States undoubtedly would be dominant, due to its industrial capacity.[48]

Within this context Levin emphasized the submarine issue as the cause most immediately responsible for drawing the United States into the conflict, an issue that illustrated better than any other the extent to which Wilson's moralism and America's national interest converged. In addition to the obvious material gains that accrued to this nation by increasing exports to the Allies, wrote Levin, "was the fact that for Wilson, the very process of defending the nation's rights on the high seas became an important aspect of America's unique liberal service to mankind." He continued that "if it was the exceptional destiny of the United States to feed, clothe, and morally instruct the world, it was also its duty to maintain the rule of law on the high seas for the benefit of all neutral trading nations." Hence, concluded Levin, "In defending America's neutral rights, then, the President was as certain as always that there was complete unity between the national interest of the United States and the values of liberal-internationalism." Given Wilson's particular perception of the world and the role that America was to play in it, it would seem he hardly could have done otherwise, which in effect was what the new revisionism suggested.[49]

What clearly bothered Levin, however, was that Wilson made little or no effort to examine the new world order from the standpoint of the needs of each of its component parts. For instance, Wilson utterly failed "to question either the structural inequitability of the commercial relationships between the agrarian and industrialized areas of the world or the correlative economic and political world predominance of the West." Had he done so he might have discovered that American solutions and models had well-nigh no applicability in the underdeveloped areas of the world. Moreover, implicit in Wilson's attempt "to construct a stable world order of liberal-capitalist internationalism, at the center of the global ideological spectrum, safe both from the threat of imperialism on the Right and the danger of Revolution on the Left" was the prohibition of revolution or violence as a legitimate vehicle for allowing the dispossessed of the world to modernize their countries and in so doing come to share in the bounty of industrial wealth. More than anything else, America's unswerving commitment to gradual change within a global open door world unnecessarily cast modern United States foreign policy into a counter-insurgency and counter-revolutionary mold, thus denying to other less fortunate peoples what, ironically enough, Wilson most cherished for them, self-determination. Only in this light could American intervention in Cuba, the Dominican Republic and Vietnam be understood today, evidencing that as late as the 1960's the Wilsonian version continued to motivate America's foreign policy leaders.[50]

Analyzing Wilsonian diplomacy from the wider angle of international politics and within the great debate surrounding belligerents' war aims in World War I, Arno J. Mayer argued in a study published in 1959 that "in Allied as well as in Central countries this issue of domestic and foreign policy became part of the struggle for power between the 'parties of order' (predominantly the Right) and the 'parties of movement' (predominantly the Left)." Generally speaking, contended Mayer, the Right favored expansionist war aims and the perpetuation of such Old Diplomacy practices as secrecy and trade restrictions as part of a concerted effort to maintain the domestic status quo, whereas the Left favored non-expansionist war aims and the adoption of such New

Diplomacy practices as open agreements openly arrived at and free trade as part of its program to alter the domestic status quo. During the course of hostilities, continued Mayer, both the Soviet Union and the United States came forward as the standard bearer of the New Diplomacy, the former from a position of weakness, the latter from a position of strength, each offering the parties of movement similar foreign-policy ideologies.

Mayer contended that, on the one hand, "Wilson counseled the Allied Governments to formulate liberal war aims in order to rekindle the fighting spirit of the Allied masses and to strengthen the enemy forces of movement undermining the political truce in the Central camp; on the other hand, Lenin sought to advance the proletarian revolution by convincing Europe's war-weary masses that it would be expedient to couple the issues of an immediate compromise peace with those of domestic reform." What did Wilson hope to achieve? Wilson, according to Mayer, invited the forces of movement of the world to join him in the experiment of building the first international commnuity that was capable of organizing change peacefully. In contrast, Lenin offered them only violent social and political revolution. In his call for a general association of nations, Wilson's ultimate objective was peace while the immediate function was the preservation of the territorial arrangements that would emerge from the Paris Peace Conference. Designed primarily as a mechanism with which to reduce and eliminate violence in an American-led world order, the League of Nations, in Mayer's framework, would "be a sort of midwife to nations about to be born; it would help them pass from the precarious stage of infancy, through adolescence, to full maturity, in a new community of power." Thus the League of Nations assumed no greater importance than the role of guardian of the American empire.[51]

In Mayer's sequel, *Politics and Diplomacy of Peace-*

making (1967), the author maintained "that whereas in
1917–18, in the heat of war, the Allied 'parties of movement' . . . put their imprint on the diplomacy of the world
crisis, in 1918–19, while peace was being made, the 'parties of order' . . . reclaimed their primacy in the victor
nations." The Republican victory in the congressional
elections of November, 1918, marked this shift in the
United States. Although it would be an exaggeration to
say that Wilson lost his power base at that time, it could
be argued that his position for securing a moderate peace
was seriously undermined. From this time forward, wrote
Mayer, "Wilson was condemned to labor in a political
field, both national and international, in which measured
reform was fatally emasculated." So far as the Versailles
Settlement was concerned, one of Wilson's major tasks at
Paris was the containment of Bolshevik Russia, an attitude commonly shared by all the victorious Allied Powers. According to Mayer's analysis, Wilson had gone to
Paris to write the ground rules of the new world order.
There, no rule received more attention than how to best
deal with the possible spread of the Soviet example to
other war-torn areas of Europe. Unable to control events
within Russia, the Allies did the next best thing: they
excluded Russia from the comity of nations. By failing
to come to terms with the Russian Revolution, the leaders of the Great Powers, Wilson among them, paved the
way for World War II. Had France been able to rely on
Russia as a counterweight to Germany, the Versailles
Settlement might have shown more leniency with the
defeated powers. The map of Europe once again had
been rearranged for the next war.[52]

Of the works under consideration, the fullest treatment
of the debate concerning the adoption of the League of
Nations in the United States was found in Carl P. Parrini's *Heir to Empire* (1969). Parrini's discussion of

Wilson's League rested on the simple assumption that "by 1916 American political and business leaders had reached the conclusion that in order to market the goods and services which the American economy was producing they had to change the rules governing trade and investment." The method used to effect the internationalization of business on the American model was the open door policy of John Hay, by which Parrini simply "meant that United States entrepreneurs ought to have the right to use their capital and managerial talents everywhere on a basis equal to that enjoyed by the businessmen of other nations." In order to realize such a world, American policy makers, averred Parrini, found it necessary to build a global commercial system that would allow American enterprise first to topple, then to replace, British business interests as the leading element in the world economy, while at the same time devising new institutional means for stabilizing the world politically. In this sense he observed that United States foreign policy from 1916 to 1929 represented a continuum. To what extent was it a continuum? "Wilson and his Republican successors," wrote Parrini, "desired an economic community of interest which the United States would manage, with the Western Europeans and Japan acting as associates with full rights in the system." In the New Left schema, that essentially was what the United States created in that period. So far as this larger goal was concerned, American foreign policy decision-makers exhibited a solid front, to the principal outlines of which they almost all agreed. First, they "had to conduct diplomacy in such a manner as to create an international political economy conducive to expansion by peaceful means"; second, "they had to give the other industrial nations of the world a real interest in the growing American direction of the world economy." The debate that followed once again concerned itself with means rather than ends.[53]

Continuing to emphasize the underlying consensus among high-ranking United States officials, Parrini noted that both "Wilson and his Republican successors shared the belief that disarmament and the open door were the twin keys to peace and community." He went on to remark, "if the world were disarmed the weapon which the United States would have at its disposal was its expanding economic power." The tactic chosen by Wilsonians to bring about this twofold aim was the League of Nations, because, in their estimate, "such a league could force disarmament and write open door rules to govern the political economy." Furthermore, he added, it was "on this tactical question [that] the American power elite split wide open," and not, as conventional accounts have asserted, the issue of isolationism versus internationalism. On this point, participants from the entire political spectrum broke with Wilson. "Men such as Herbert Hoover, Charles Evans Hughes, Philander C. Knox, Henry L. Stimson, and William Howard Taft, and Elihu Root to a greater or lesser extent, concluded that Wilson's Article 10 of the League of Nations Covenant was too inflexible to achieve real disarmament or generate the pressure to widen successively the application of the open door to ever larger areas of the world. Moreover, they believed that American participation in the League would deprive the United States of the freedom to use its economic power."

In arguing against the League, anti-Wilsonians perceived that United States participation in such an organization placed American foreign policy in a straight jacket. To have participated in it would in effect have meant, first, that America acquiesced "in a British-managed closed door world, since England had already taken much of the political and economic lead on the Continent and various clauses of the Versailles Treaty (and politically lesser but significant treaties with Turkey and the Succession states) had given Britain special positions in Central and Eastern Europe"; in the second place, it would have "imposed a moral obligation on American statesmen to accept—and even take joy in— a world they never made, and which they saw as soil for seeds of another war"; and in the third and last place it needlessly "substituted the principle of force, labeled Collective Security, for the practice of allowing political conflicts, largely held to be based on economic competition, to work themselves out through the principle of the real open door." Wilson and his supporters could not have disagreed more.[54]

Wilsonians held, for example, that a community of powers acting in concert could not be realized without Article 10. They believed, wrote Parrini, "a League based on Article 10 would guarantee that future wars would only be fought to preserve the peace." As both Levin and Mayer suggested, the mandate system would be regarded as a means of encouraging economic and political independence for underdeveloped countries without resort to revolution. Seen in another light, Wilsonians hoped to oulaw violence as a legitimate method of effecting change. In regard to which side was "right," Parrini came out squarely for Wilson's opposition. In the author's estimate, "Had the United States joined the League of Nations in 1920 the European powers undoubtedly would have been in a position to nail shut the door in many areas of the world, while at the same time adhering to a formal recognition of the open door out of deference to President Wilson." Whatever the relative merits of arguments for and against the League, Parrini's study implied the principle of a stable open door world was in itself faulty. The problem with a policy of this nature, suggested Parrini within the context of discussing Wilson's "new world order" as a counterpoise to "the poison of Bolshevism," was that it willy-nilly placed the United States in the business of counterrevolution. Upheaval anywhere, and for any reason, became the nation's business. However much America might imagine it necessary in serving its own interests, both ideologically and materially, suppression of revolutionary tendencies hardly was a first step toward building a world community. Rather, concluded Parrini, it could only be seen as the first step toward wasted resources which could better be used to build a true community both in the United States and abroad.[55]

As to the interwar years and the coming of World War II, the new revisionism—in contrast to orthodox interpretations which argued that with the rejection of the League of Nations the United States turned inward and indulged itself in isolationist policies until the threat of totalitarianism became so great that common sense dictated it must be resisted now or at some time in the future —contended that American leaders continued to think and act in terms of implementing an open door world. In *Economic Aspects of New Deal Diplomacy* (1965), for example, Lloyd C. Gardner held that in general "the New Deal's approach to foreign affairs was as much shaped by older principles and traditions as by any initiated by Franklin Roosevelt, who, after all, had also grown up believing in such important American policies as that of the Asian Open Door."

Faced with the enormous problem of propping up a tottering economy, leaders of the 1930's, like all United States policy makers since the turn of the century, had two basic alternatives before them. They could, as others had done, continue to pursue a policy of continued commercial expansion within the framework of an open door world, and thus, in New Left terms, continue to export the social problem. The alternative was pursuit of a policy of economic nationalism, a form of "self-containment," which implied, among other things, coming to terms with the structural faults inherent in the overdevelopment of America's political economy. "How to make a choice between the two," wrote Gardner, "was the crisis of the new order." Franklin Roosevelt's early economic nationalism, revealed by the so-called "bombshell message" to the World Economic Conference meeting in London, held out hope that America would attempt to come to terms with itself through a domestic solution. But "after a momentary pause," observed Gardner, "New Deal foreign policy rejoined the mainstream in 1934 with the adoption of the Reciprocal Trade Agreements Act," replete with the most-favored-nation clause. Thus, according to the New Left model, New Deal policy makers set out to implement the goal of equality of commercial opportunity implicit in maintaining a freely trading open door world which would guarantee markets for America's surplus goods and capital while at the same time insuring easy access to the raw materials of the world. For Gardner, then, there could be little doubt that "the years before . . . World War II demonstrated that the United States regarded the defense of its liberal foreign policy as central to its conduct of its foreign policy and the stem of the policy's ideology."[56]

Regarding the increasing threat of totalitarianism to world peace in the 1930's, the danger posed by Hitlerian Germany, Gardner noted that after 1937 American policy makers indeed were fearful of the Axis' apparent conspiracy to dominate the globe. The key to understanding American attitudes, however, was that this fear was not motivated only by opposition to the evilness of

Nazism. To be sure, wrote Gardner, Hitler's challenge "was a total challenge, but it was not the existence of Nazism *per se* that made World War II and American entrance into that struggle inevitable; rather it was the expansion of the system." That Hitler posed a serious and very real military threat to the security of the United States could not be gainsaid. What often has been overlooked, according to the new revisionism, was that "Nazi Germany's autarkic economic policies were far more serious to American leaders than has been assumed." To what extent were they serious? "Germany's economic competition in South America constantly kept Washington on edge; nor should it be passed over that Washington's views on Germany were consistent with its outlook on the rest of the world." Reasoning in such a manner, Gardner attempted above all "to call attention to the fact that American policy was not just a reaction to German or Japanese militarism," pointing out that the conflict between them "was a much older struggle going back to 1900 and always broadly speaking, about the open door policy." The United States feared that its interests and influence shortly were to be expelled from both Europe and the Far East. Whether the United States would have gone to war with Japan and Germany if it had never heard of the open door and was in an economic sense "self-contained, Gardner does not venture to say. All he could say for certain was that "in Manchuria (before, during, and after the war), in the Middle East, in Latin America, in fact nearly everywhere, the United States wanted the open door policy and an open world." The reader was left to draw his own conclusions.[57]

Like Gardner, Robert Freeman Smith rejected the conventional "view of a somewhat befuddled, defensive United States facing a world of predatory aggressors, and

instead present[ed] the United States as a rather imperial-minded power with ambitions and goals which on
the whole are rather similar to those of most powers."
Placing New Deal diplomacy within the context of the
open-door world outlook that supposedly had informed
American foreign policy in the interwar years, Smith
rejected outright the orthodox description of the United
States in the interwar years as an innocent onlooker
whose foreign policy was being made in the other capi-
tals of the world while at-home policy makers indulged
themselves in isolationist fantasies. On the contrary, argued Smith, "One of the basic concerns of United States
policy makers from 1920 to 1941 was the establishment
and maintenance of a world order which would be conducive to the prosperity and power of the United States,"
a project of American leaders perfectly consistent with
"beliefs concerning mission and destiny and faith in the
humanitarian nature of United States goals." Smith did
not doubt the success of the United States efforts for,
like Parrini, he argued that "by 1929 the United States
seemed largely to have achieved the goal of an open
door world order." It was in this setting, concluded Smith,
that American-Axis relations must be examined and the
essentially self-interested nature of American foreign
policy assessed. When the Axis powers threatened to
dismantle that structure, the United States decided to
resist, by persuasion if possible, by force if necessary.
That the United States would find it necessary to continue
that struggle after the defeat of the Axis powers came as
no surprise to the New Left.[58]

4. ORIGIN OF THE COLD WAR

The View from the New Left

"Historians of the fifties," remarked Norman A. Graebner recently, "tended to accept the Cold War orthodoxy laid down by United States and British officials in speeches, writings, memoirs, communications, and recorded conversations between 1945 and 1950." More specifically, he continued, "Such writers accepted the notion of Soviet aggression as valid and of Western firmness as necessary. They accepted the logic of United States containment policy and regarded it generally as the most successful of the nation's postwar decisions both in concept and expectation." Furthermore, in almost all these conventional accounts, Soviet responsibility for starting the Cold War was assumed and seldom, if ever, questioned. Herbert Feis, eminent among traditional Cold War scholars, declared: "Some of our schemes may well have called on the Soviet government for excessive effort and resources compared to the anticipated military result; and some others carelessly brushed Soviet pride." After factoring out American insensibilities, however, wrote Feis, one must conclude that "Soviet actions evi-

denced an unwillingness to trust the outcome of the
democratic political contest, and a ruthless will to make
sure that all of Central and Eastern Europe was governed by its independent supporters"; for, in the final
analysis, "the Soviet Union wanted space, satellite peoples and armies, additional economic resources, and a
favorable chance for communism to spread its influence."

State Department official Joseph M. Jones evinced a
similarly held belief, probably the opinion of the majority
of his colleagues. "The Soviet Union, unique in its power
position in two continents," wrote Jones in 1955, "had
demonstrated beyond any doubt that it was aggressive
and expanding, and that its immediate design for domin-
ion included as much of Europe and North Africa as it
could get away with short of war with its Western allies."

From another perspective, Kremlinologist Adam B.
Ulam placed primary responsibility for the coming of the
Cold War on the Soviet system itself. Ulam reached the
judgment that, while there was an occasional American
communications problem with Soviet policy makers in
general and with Stalin in particular, there could be little
doubt that "whatever his feeling [of gratitude and hope
toward Churchill and Franklin Roosevelt] Stalin could
not in the long run withstand the logic of his position as
the ruler of a totalitarian society and as the supreme head
of a movement that seeks security through constant expansion. In these facts more than in any sins of omission
or commission by the West must be seen the seeds of the
growing discords of the cold war."[59]

In the years that followed, other scholarly American
writers and commentators, who for the sake of this
discussion may be regarded as moderate revisionists,
attempted to place the postwar struggle of the two super-
powers within the concept of what English historian
Herbert Butterfield once called the "terrible human pre-

dicament: "a situation in which even intelligent and reasonably well-intentioned men move inexorably toward conflict. Historian and diplomat Louis J. Halle, for example, sought to capture that dilemma in the since-famous image of the scorpion and the tarantula in a bottle: "If you put a scorpion and a tarantula in a bottle the objective of their own self-preservation will impel them to fight each other to the death." From another perspective, he went on to say, "The historical circumstances themselves had an ineluctable quality that left the Russians little choice but to move as they did." America was thrown on the defensive because given the decision of Soviet foreign-policy makers to thrust outward, the United States was compelled to respond. In this way, concluded Halle, "the Cold War was joined." Even Dexter Perkins, who had not the slightest reservation about what he conceived to be the essential wickedness of communism and the hostility of Soviet foreign policy, doubted that the Cold War could have been avoided. Given the bipolar nature of the postwar world and the rival dreams that underlay the motives of each power, conflict was inherent in the situation. "The position, the interests and the ideals of the United States and the Soviet Union," maintained Perkins, "were opposed to one another; today it seems almost inconceivable that any formula could have been found that would reconcile them. If anything is ever inevitable, the clash of these two powers was inevitable."[60]

Whatever the differences that separated them, traditionalists and moderate revisionists agreed that Soviet aggression lay at the heart of the Cold War. Whether that aggressiveness was powered by fear and security, the time-honored goals of Tsarist expansionism, or by the Soviet system of government itself, all agreed that the Soviet Union had only itself to blame for the intensity and duration of the Cold War. The New Left diplomatic historiography that emerged in the 1960's nearly reversed that picture, holding the Soviets on the defensive and American "aggression" responsible for the near-catastrophes and bitterness that marked the postwar era. Driven by the structural dynamics of America's inherently expansionistic capitalist political economy and by an American idealism that casually transformed itself into a missionary anticommunism, the United States after World War II, according to the New Left model, sought to create a freely trading open door world conductive to securing markets for American surpluses on the one hand and importing vitally needed raw materials on the other.

Americans sincerely believed that from such a world democratic institutions and practices would flow, satisfying at once both American interests and ideals. The pursuit of such an open door world, ran the New Left argument, failed to recognize the needs and desires of the Soviet Union. Such recognition would have meant supplying the wherewithal for economic reconstruction and establishing an Eastern European sphere of interest or zone of security to guard against yet a third German invasion in this century. When America could have helped most, and presumably assuaged Soviet fears, it helped least, demanding the removal of the iron curtain or any other obstruction that threatened to impede the functioning of an open door world. If there was anything tragic, inevitable or ineluctable about the Cold War, it was that the structure, institutions and traditions of this nation's political ·economy made it so. Furthermore, unless Americans desisted from identifying their prosperity and well-being with the search for expanding markets in an open door world, the remainder of twentieth-century American diplomacy could expect to be no more than a repetition of the Cold War experience, i.e., continued near-catastrophes, bitterness and perhaps the nuclear holocaust itself.

The purpose of the following remarks is to provide a critical examination of major New Left interpretations of the Cold War, focusing mainly on the published writing of Gar Alperovitz, Walter LaFeber, Gabriel Kolko and Lloyd C. Gardner. Within this framework the narrative will address itself to the following questions: What does the New Left conceive to be the principle issue of the Cold War? What is the nature of alleged American aggression, and to what extent did it influence Soviet foreign policy? What course did American diplomacy take and what course could it have taken to avoid a falling out with its erstwhile rival? In what way does the New Left critique of the Cold War differ from preceding interpretations? What similarities, if any, do they share? To what extent do New Left diplomatic historians differ from one another? To what degree do their analyses reflect similarities?

Utilizing William Appleman Williams's model of an ambitious America striving to create a global open door in the post-World War II period, Gar Alperovitz argued in *Atomic Diplomacy* (1965) and in a number of related essays that, given the nature of United States foreign policy, there was nothing particularly tragic or inevitable about the Cold War, and that, if any nation should be attributed with starting the conflict, it should be the United States. In analyzing the connection between American acquisition of the atomic bomb and the foreign policy of Harry S. Truman, Alperovitz theorized that far from following Franklin Roosevelt's "policy of cooperation, . . . Truman launched a powerful foreign policy initiative aimed at reducing or eliminating Soviet influence from Europe."

"I believe," wrote Alperovitz of Secretary of War Henry L. Stimson's diary, "new evidence proves not only that the atomic bomb influenced diplomacy, but that it determined much of Truman's shift to a policy aimed at forcing Soviet acquiescence to American plans for Eastern and Central Europe." Alperovitz's observation was not in itself innovative, for it is a truism that all historical debate is rooted in the past. D. F. Fleming, an embittered Wilsonian internationalist, noted in a vigorous minority dissent published in 1961 that with the rough handling of Soviet Foreign Minister Molotov on April 23, 1945, eleven days after Roosevelt's death, Truman reversed "the entire Roosevelt-Hull approach to Russia and inaugurated an era of toughness in our dealings with Russia." What separated these two accounts, however, was Alperovitz's heavy emphasis on economic motives, although the idealism of American foreign policy by no means was ignored.[61]

According to Alperovitz, by the third week of April, 1945, President Truman and his advisers believed the time had come to reconsider what the new revisionism generally assumed to have been Roosevelt's policy of cooperation with the Soviet Union. Why was the third week of April chosen? What would Roosevelt have done differently? "For most of the war," wrote Alperovitz in a related context, "Roosevelt had been highly ambivalent toward such motives. By late 1945, however, in spite of wavering on the politically sensitive Polish issue in his dying days, Roosevelt concluded it would be a fundamental error to put too much pressure on Russia regarding other regimes vital to her security." Moreover, he continued, "In September and October, 1944, and in early 1945, he gave form to his conclusion by entering into armistice agreements with Britain and Russia, which gave the Soviet military almost complete control of internal politics in each Eastern European ex-Nazi satellite," in a real sense formalizing "the famous Churchill-Stalin spheres of influence arrangement." More importantly, suggested Alperovitz, and by implication what most orthodox accounts tended to ignore, was that "The armistice accords were also modeled after a previous understanding that had contained Soviet endorsement of dominant American-British influence in Italy." Truman and his advisers, at the very least, should have recognized the *quid pro quo* basis of postwar territorial arrangements; at most, they should have continued to work with the Russians on this principle. In Alperovitz's reconstruction of events, Roosevelt, for two important reasons, had little alternative but to cooperate with Stalin. First, Roosevelt clearly discerned the then-current mood of American public opinion which insisted on quick demobilization, making it impossible to retain a large number of United States forces in Europe after the war; second, Roosevelt believed he needed the Red Army to guarantee that a revived Germany would not rise phoenix-like from the ashes. "And," wrote Alperovitz, "whatever his [Roosevelt's] personal wishes, such a guarantee was a self-evident political necessity in 1945. . . . Stalin also needed American help, as he too made clear, to hold down the Germans." Nonetheless, continued Alperovitz, there was always the possibility that "Roosevelt might have chosen to press the traditional objective [of an American-led open door world] on Eastern Europe, but he would not have had the military power to back them up if at any point his bluff were called. And he would have risked losing Soviet cooperation in Germany." This was Roosevelt's position until the day he died.[62]

What subsequently changed was President Truman's attitude toward acquisition of an incipient atomic arsenal. "When approached in power terms," contended Alperovitz, "Truman's changes [in foreign policy] later in 1945 are not difficult to understand: the central difference was the existence of the newly developed atom bomb, which Roosevelt, who died on April 12, 1945, simply could not count on." Thus, in a single stroke, according to Alperovitz's thesis, the bomb removed—or so Truman imagined—the constraints that previously had limited Roosevelt's policy. In the first place, he argued, "It was no longer necessary to have more troops in order to implement the policy [or the open door] in Eastern Europe"; in the second place, "the bomb meant that *the United States could handle the German problem by itself.*" From this point forward the United States both could guard against a revived Germany in the future without Soviet assistance and could intimidate Stalin from drawing an iron curtain down on an exclusive Soviet sphere of interest.[63]

Assuming, among other things, that American interests required active influence in East and Central Europe, Truman and his foreign-policy makers exhibited unanimity about the goal; the only question seriously debated was which strategy best could serve that end. The two strategies ultimately chosen were those of immediate and delayed showdown with the Soviets. Advocates of immediate showdown, with W. Averell Harriman, American Ambassador in Moscow, in the forefront, selected Poland as a symbolic showdown. This strategy miserably failed either to force the restructuring of the Lublin government or to dent the Kremlin's determination to make "friendly neighbors" of traditionally Russian-hating Poles. Related to this strategy, such other tactics as economic leverage—abrupt stoppage of Lend-Lease shipments to Russia and officially feigned ignorance of Molotov's request in early 1945 for a postwar loan (which was finally rejected after the Potsdam meeting)—were employed, but to no avail. Having failed in this approach, Truman adopted the delayed-showdown strategy of Secretary of War Henry L. Stimson.

A great conservative and a consummate realist, Stimson, according to Alperovitz, hoped it would be possible "to preserve American economic interests in Eastern Europe," but "he took for granted Soviet special interests in the border countries just as he accepted American special interests in Latin America." Unlike the majority of Truman's advisers, Stimson believed that Soviet cooperation was the *sine qua non* of postwar stability in Europe and that some sort of *modus vivendi* would have to be worked out with the Kremlin on the border lands of Russia. Stimson's reason in the spring of 1945 for delaying a showdown with Stalin until the summer's Potsdam meeting was that, according to Alperovitz, "the atomic bomb would add great power to American diplomacy once it was developed. He considered that no major issue could be realistically discussed without an estimate of the bomb's role," a point that even Alperovitz's severest critics have conceded. For this reason, Stimson deemed it of the utmost importance that a showdown with the Soviets be postponed. Alperovitz quoted Stimson as having written in his diary: " 'We shall probably hold more cards in our hand later than now.' " By no means, however, did Alperovitz suggest that Stimson hoped at that time to extort concessions from the Russians. On the contrary, Alperovitz repeatedly contended that Stimson's single most important wish was to win their cooperation by "urging them that the secret of the weapon be offered as a bargaining counter." This shift in tactics, ran the thesis, explained the Hopkins Mission to Moscow and renewal of Lend-Lease shipments that had been in transit; in short, stalling for time.[64]

A related political objective of the Truman administration was to keep the Soviet Army out of the Far East, i.e., obviating the necessity of Stalin's fulfilling his pledge given at Yalta that the Soviet Union would declare war against Japan approximately three months after the war in Europe ended. "American policy makers," wrote Alperovitz, "aware that Russia could conquer the Japa-- nese armies in the China mainland in less than two months, desperately hoped to end the war before Soviet military operations paved the way for domination of Manchuria and North China," long a bone of contention in America's open door policy in the Far East. If Japan's defeat was inevitable and clearly foreseen in the summer of 1945, as Alperovitz himself argued, why did Truman ignore the possibility of ending the war with Japan sooner? "It was *assumed*—not decided—the bomb would be used," declared Alperovitz. So, and here the thrust of the Alperovitz study lay, the decision to use the atomic bomb against Japan was of a more political than a military nature, the ultimate purpose of which was to intimidate the Kremlin to acquiesce in the American goal of a global open door by a combat demonstration on an all-but-defeated enemy. Contrasted to the traditional interpretation that dropping the atomic bomb was necessary to shock the Japanese into accepting unconditional surrender terms, Alperovitz's analysis contended that the bomb served the dual purpose, first, of attempting to keep the Soviet Union out of the war against Japan and, second, of generally strengthening the hand of the United States at the diplomatic conference shortly to be convened at Potsdam. Alperovitz quoted Stimson as having said, "Laying it [the atomic bomb] on Japan would be necessary to impress a man such as Stalin."[65]

The strategy of delayed showdown obviously did not seem to work. It did not prevent the Soviets from declaring war against the Japanese and occupying large areas of the Far East. Nonetheless, Truman went his own way, declaring that the United States alone would occupy Japan. China was assured that the Russians would keep their agreement in regard to Manchuria. And Stalin did. By the end of July, Truman, according to Alperovitz, discarded the Stimson concept of the secret weapon as a bargaining counter with the Soviets and adopted in its place the temporary monopoly concept of Secretary of State James F. Byrnes, using the atomic bomb as a potential threat with which to browbeat the Soviet Union into submission. Taking up the offensive, Truman demanded that the governments of East and Central Europe be restructured and that prewar American interests be guaranteed. Stalin, for his own reasons, refused to yield. When Molotov again refused to yield on the issue of the then-current composition of the Bulgarian and Rumanian governments at the Council of Foreign Ministers meeting in London in September, 1945, the Cold War could be said to have begun. In this and in innumerable other instances, concluded Alperovitz, "The atomic bomb profoundly influenced the way American policy makers viewed political problems." Rather than producing American opposition to Soviet moves in Eastern Europe and the Far East, which by definition of the American open door world would have been opposed in any event by the majority of policy makers, "the atomic bomb confirmed American leaders in their judgment that they had sufficient power to affect developments in the broader regions of the Soviet Union." Alperovitz emphasized: "The decision to use the weapon did not derive from overriding military considerations" to defeat the already beaten Japanese, but rather derived from the majority judgment that "a combat demonstration was needed to convince the Russians to accept the American plan for a stable peace." Here lay the origin of the Cold War.[66]

Although they commonly shared the belief that United States foreign policy may best be understood as an ongoing function of America's capitalistic political economy, a number of New Left historians took exception to what they believed to be Alperovitz's undue emphasis on immediate postwar diplomacy. Gabriel Kolko, who in any discussion of the new revisionism must be placed at the extreme left of the political spectrum, disagreed with Alperovitz, maintaining that the emergence of Truman to the Presidency in no way marked a fundamental departure from the preceding administration. "Harry S. Truman," wrote Kolko in 1968, "retained all of Roosevelt's key advisers, who by and large continued to direct policy for the rest of the war." Moreover, he suggested, it would be a mistake to attribute Roosevelt himself with any external policy at all, for at no time during World War II did Roosevelt "lead or define American foreign policy." The real leader of foreign policy, which in any case was economically motivated, was Cordell Hull, Roosevelt's Secretary of State from 1933 to 1944. Turning conventional interpretations upside down, Kolko declared, "That Hull was a minor figure under Roosevelt is a myth without basis in fact." Furthermore, he wrote, the attitude to be taken toward the Soviets would be determined not by what the Soviets wanted, but by what the implementation of America's economic war aims would allow the Soviets to have.

Kolko also failed to agree with the "atomic diplomacy" thesis that with the acquisition of atomic bombs United States policy makers frantically hurried to defeat Japan in order to foreclose on the Russian pretext to enter the conflict. From the beginning, contended Kolko, Stimson "and most of the leaders in Washington wanted to make surrender easier for Japan to keep the Russians out of the homeland of the enemy itself. This distinction was critical and never altered." From another perspective, Kolko said, "Soviet entry into the war itself was never contingent on American approval, and it could not be stopped." At all times, he added, "the Russians were fighting in their own self-interest and this was the prevalent view in Washington." Besides, "It was hardly necessary for the Americans to drop two bombs on Japan to exhibit the destructive power of the weapon to the Russians, and this was never the intention." From their own research and sources of information the Soviets knew full well what the atomic bomb could and was expected to do. Kolko noted that the only possible way the Alperovitz thesis could be valid was if one granted the assumption that American policy makers were prepared to obliterate the cities of their erstwhile ally. This, he concluded, could not be taken seriously for the period under consideration, although he has no doubt that it subsequently was considered a possibility.[67]

Like Kolko, Lloyd C. Gardner disagreed with Alperovitz's approach toward explaining events in the immediate postwar period, especially the assertion that once in office Truman launched his own foreign policy offensive. In the first place, wrote Gardner, "By beginning the book after Roosevelt's death he asks questions that pertain only to immediate decisions, not to larger ones"; the evidence suggested "that both Roosevelt and Truman had a primary concern to establish a new world order." Thus, each man pursuing the same open door world would have encountered the same opposition from the Soviets, and the Cold War would inevitably have been joined. That much seemed certain.[68]

In *America, Russia, and the Cold War, 1945-1966* (1967), the second of the major New Left interpretations of the Cold War under consideration, Walter LaFeber attempted to show that Truman's efforts to

penetrate the iron curtain in the immediate postwar
period was symptomatic of the twentieth-century American policy of resisting exclusive trading practices everywhere. "Since becoming a major power," wrote LaFeber,
"the United States had viewed anything resembling
Stalin's fence as incompatible with American objectives."
In this nation's traditional pursuit of a freely trading
open door world which would receive its ever-growing
surplus goods and capital, divisions of this nature were
ipso facto to be resisted. Whether speaking of the Ro-
manovs or the Bolsheviks, "Russia had historically been
a chief offender in this regard." In this sense the Cold
War had almost a preordained quality about it.[69]

Immediate causes of the Cold War, suggested LaFeber,
lay "in stalling the second front invasion until 1944" and
in refusing to assure him [Stalin] that after the conflict
the Soviet borders essentially would be those recognized
by the Nazi-Soviet treaty, viz., that the Baltic states and
parts of Poland, Finland, and Rumania would be ab-
sorbed by Russia. LaFeber's analysis of Cold War origins rested essentially on four assumptions. First, wrote
LaFeber, "Washington officials . . . assumed that foreign
policy grew directly from domestic policy; American
actions abroad did not respond primarily to the pressures
of other nations, but to political, social, and economic
forces at home." Of these, emphasized LaFeber in a
manner illustrative of his entire approach to Cold War
origins, "Policy makers could consider the economic the
most important . . . a not unreasonable conclusion given
the national crisis endured in the 1930's."

Second was the looming spectre of depression. "The
ghosts of Depression Past and Depression Future," wrote
LaFeber, "led officials to a second assumption" that "the
post-1929 quagmire had been prolonged and partly
caused by high tariff walls and regional trading blocs

which had dammed up the natural flow of foreign trade."
Policy makers reasoned that above all else "such economic dislocation led to political conflicts which, in turn,
had ignited World War." In the new world order that was
expected to follow, and in the light of recent history,
Washington concluded that "free flow of exports and
imports was essential." The third assumption was that,
this time, the United States was in a position to avoid
the mistakes of the past. By "quadrupling its production
while other major industrial nations suffered severe wartime damage," the United States "wielded the requisite
economic power to establish this desired economic
community."

The fourth and final assumption of LaFeber's analysis
was the presumed determination of "Washington policy
makers . . . to use this type of gigantic economic power."
Thus in LaFeber's model of Cold War diplomacy—and
the same may be said of New Left diplomatic literature
as a whole—one drew the conclusion that United States
foreign policy may be explained or interpreted as an
ongoing function of the nation's capitalist political economy, a political economy whose structural dynamics required an open door commercial empire for the export
of America's surplus goods and capital on the one hand
and the import of vitally needed raw materials on the
other. Fearing depression and the consequence of solving its own problem of overdevelopment, which presumably would necessitate a radical societal reordering
or, at least, the establishing of some sort of nonexpanding society, America pushed outward as a solution to
what should have been regarded an internal problem.
What opposition the United States faced in the postwar
world came neither from ideologically expansive world
communism with its headquarters in Moscow nor from a
failure to reach a *modus vivendi* with the Soviets in the

new balance of power being born, but rather from the resistance encountered to America's blind pursuit to remake the world in terms and definition of its own meaning. To look for the provenance of the Cold War in the Kremlin was simply to bypass the issue.[70]

LaFeber evinced little admiration for the course and quality of Soviet foreign policy, although he went to considerable length to empathize with the Russian position. "With considerably more brutality," wrote LaFeber, "Joseph Stalin also constructed his postwar policies upon the necessity of maintaining freedom of action in spheres he considered vital for economic and strategic requirements." LaFeber said, "Regardless of the threat, whether economic or atomic, Stalin had reasons for not lifting the curtain. For strategic and psychological purposes, he divided Germany and then maintained buffer states between Germany and the Soviet Union." The fear of German revival, according to the New Left model, dominated Stalin's thinking. To be sure, wrote LaFeber, "Doctrinal demands and neurotic personal ambition partly explained Stalin's policies in this area"; but more significantly, "the overriding requirement dictating this policy was the Soviet need for security and economic reconstruction."[71]

LaFeber pictured Stalin caught on the horns of a dilemma. On the one hand, he wrote, "If he wished quick economic reconstruction he would need American funds, since the United States possessed the only sufficient capital supply in the world"; on the other hand, "to obtain these funds . . . Stalin would have to loosen his control of Eastern Europe, allow American political and economic power to flow into the area, and consequently surrender what he considered to be the first essential of Soviet security." Stalin could have one or the other, but apparently not both. In the final analysis, wrote LaFeber,

"Stalin imposed a communist system over most of these areas, not because the historical inevitability of Karl Marx had come to pass, but because in the Russian's view, both the security and economic requirements could be found in such a system, and the success of the Red Army presented a unique opportunity to act." With each power moving inexorably in its own way, the conflict between the United States and the Soviet Union in the postwar period assumed an almost tragic quality. "For American policy makers dedicated to creating a Western democratic world built on the Atlantic Charter Freedoms, Stalin's move posed the terrible problem of how to open the Soviet empire without alienating the Soviets," LaFeber pointed out. Given their *Weltanschauung* United States foreign policy leaders had little alternative but to resist Soviet efforts to carve out an exclusive sphere of interest. In this dilemma, concluded LaFeber, lay the course of the Cold War.[72]

Moving beyond traditional critiques of post-World War II American diplomacy, which had come under especial scrutiny of such Realists as Kennan and Morgenthau, LaFeber concerned himself chiefly with the source of American diplomacy. LaFeber viewed the basis of modern foreign policy as a conscious attempt since the late nineteenth century to create an American commercial empire. In their efforts to construct this empire by means of a freely trading liberal capitalist world, Americans unnecessarily preoccupied themselves with such matters as "stability, peace, and confidence in the sanctity of contract." Developing into an industrial giant, seeking outlets for its surpluses and attempting to create a world order in which it could thrive and prosper, "the United States," according to this model, "had burgeoned into a power which combined the interesting characteristics of being conservative ideologically and expansive economically." In the process Americans conveniently forgot their own revolutionary beginnings and sought to deny to other, less fortunate, peoples perhaps the only suitable vehicle of reform left to them, violence. In denying violent revolution as a legitimate vehicle of reform, the United States, for the most part, denied the validity of reform itself, the effects of which may be felt in American intervention throughout the underdeveloped Third World. Further, without structural and institutional reordering at home, Americans could expect more of the same, more Cubas and Vietnams. This was the essence of LaFeber's message, the heart of the new revisionism.[73]

The theme of Gabriel Kolko's *The Politics of War* (1968), which in a number of ways continued the story begun by Arno J. Mayer, was that "the primary condition of World War II, the crucial background for understanding *all* else, was the unprecedented human pain and misery, the millions upon millions of deaths, the widespread tragedy and suffering transforming the existence of peoples of Europe and Asia, tragedy and torment the depths of which no one however sensitive can plumb." The prewar social structure had collapsed under the weight of the consequences of World War II.

"The war," argued Kolko in another metaphor, "swept away all the institutions and relationships that anchor man to his society: the home was shattered, the family destroyed, work was gone, hunger and danger were ever more pressing as ever growing millions wandered over lands in search of safety and security, or as enemies or governments forcibly wrenched them from their environment." Perhaps more importantly, he continued, "Man became degraded and uprooted, and having lost his commitment to an interest in conventional ways and wisdom, he sought to redeem himself and his society in order to save himself." From this standpoint, American policy makers completely failed to recognize that "the impact of World War II on the individuals who experienced and fortunately survived it was the motor of political and social change, the creator of mass movements and parties, the catalyst that made men act, that destroyed constituted order everywhere." Kolko concluded, "All who wished to survive accepted in principle the currency of violence and repression, for it was the reality that had transformed their existence and one which they could not deny." No situation or set of circumstances could be further removed from the stable open-door world of American liberal capitalism.[74]

During the period from 1943 to 1945 and within the context of the upheaval that accompanied World War II, three major issues dominated the thinking of United States foreign-policy makers. "First," wrote Kolko, "was the question of the Left, which is to say, the disintegration of the prewar social system and the growth of revolutionary movements and potential upheaval everywhere in the world." Second, he continued, "was the problem of the Soviet Union, which at the time appeared very much concerned with the issue of the Left . . . finally, there was the issue of Great Britain, invariably set in the context of the future of the world economy and its present and future relationship to the United States." With these issues foremost in their minds, American policy makers made plans for the postwar world.[75]

American planning for the postwar period became based on two general premises, one economic and the other political. Policy makers assumed that from an economic standpoint, the character of World War II was of an exceptional nature; they assumed secondly that from a political standpoint, the United States would be the leader of those states which had constituted the prewar

European capitalist order. "The major premise of the unusually sophisticated war planning that went into United States economic peace aims," according to Kolko, "was that World War II was an exceptional incident in the history of world capitalism, and not the beginning of its end"; a second and related premise was "the political assumption . . . that the great capitalist states and their prewar spheres of influence would re-emerge from the war as powers America could control and reform, and not that the war had irrevocably weakened the prewar order." Within this world order-to-be the United States naturally assumed that Great Britain and Germany would play roles of economic competitors but capitalist allies and that both before long would achieve prewar industrial strength. By implication other nations that opposed the American plan would either be co-opted or resisted.[76]

Turning to American preparations for reconstructing the world economy, Kolko noted that, while "emergency reconstruction and relief problems would exist," for the most part "they would be temporary and solved essentially as a product of the creation of a rational world economy, based on economic liberalism and the open door that assumed the general interest of the world was synonymous with that of the United States. Put another way, America sought to create a "Hullian" world, an economic order based on the world outlook of Cordell Hull. The Hullian view, stated simply, comprised a rationally ordered international economic system, with a minimum of tariff and state economic barriers, and easy access to raw materials of the world. It embraced all the essentials of America's historic pursuit of a freely trading open door world, based on equality of commercial opportunity, in which America readily could find foreign markets for its surplus goods and capital while keeping open channels of vitally needed raw materials. The immediate force powering the American economic drive, without an understanding of which United States postwar planning was unintelligible, was fear of an iminent depression. This fear of depression, which appears in one form or another in almost all New Left Cold War literature, Kolko attributed to Americans' collective awareness in regard "to the vastly increased industrial capacity that the economy would have to deal with during the period of transition to peace." To the extent that a man's environment predetermines the manner in which he will react to a given set of circumstances, American postwar planners found themselves obliged to defend a twofold commitment "to the objectives of containment and stability—containment of the dual menace of the Left and Soviet Union, and stability for the essential social and economic system of prewar European capitalism and colonialism." Guardian of international law and order and leader of world capitalism, the United States had in effect taken on the world for its domain.[77]

Driven by its own objectives, the United States, continued Kolko's argument, mistakenly misread the sources of Soviet foreign policy conduct, seeing an ideological war ahead where none existed. What did Stalin want? In Kolko's words, "Stalin, if nothing else, was a consummate realist who based his actions on a keen awareness of the limits and possibilities of real power in being," and was the exponent "of sheer pragmatism." There could be little doubt that "by October 1944, the Soviet Union was pursuing a pluralistic policy in Eastern Europe based on the specific political conditions in each country." Blinded once again by the glare of Bolshevism, United States policy makers overlooked what should have been obvious: "The problem of estimating Russian intentions began when Americans failed to make a distinction between the USSR as a state and the Internationalist Bolshevik ideology to which Russia gave obeisance, and about which Communists spoke on May Day," averred Kolko. In consequence of such reasoning, "All the Western fears of revolution, now personified in the dynamics of an emergent New Left and Resistance, they projected on the Russians."

Given the bugbear of an international communist conspiracy prepared to embark on world conquest, the United States saw Soviet-led communists everywhere. "The 1917-vintage Bulgarians and the partisans in the Croatian mountains," wrote Kolko sardonically, "all seemed mysteriously linked to the Kremlin and responsive to it. With this view, of course, the Americans confused any small nation's act of friendship toward the Russians with an oath of fealty, and they might dismiss neutral leaders, as they did Benes [of Czechoslovakia], as having been lured by the sirens of Moscow." More importantly, and often overlooked in conventional Cold War interpretations, the Soviets seemed fully alive to such American fears. The Soviet Union, indicated Kolko, clearly "understood . . . the risks of any covert aid to the Left, and gave precious little of it during and immediately after the war, when they discovered that even an obviously conservative policy failed to blunt the American belief that behind all the world's social and economic ills, somehow, and in some critical fashion, a Russian plot and device existed." What in part had happened was that within the view provided by the dual preoccupation with containment and stability, "United States policy makers saw Russia and the Left as the cause rather than the reflection of the collapse of capitalism, and responsible for the failings of a system that began to commit suicide in vast areas of the globe no later than 1914."

There was an ironic aspect to American confusion over the allegedly sinister connection between Soviet intentions and leftist movements. According to Kolko, "It was Soviet conservatism on revolutionary movement everywhere that gave Western European capitalism the critical breathing spell during which it might [and did] recover, though the caution of the Western European Communist parties became a permanent and willingly self-imposed fact of life." Ironically, Western European capitalists owed their success to Stalin's Soviet brand of communism.[78]

Whatever the intention of Stalin, American foreign policy decision-makers sought to realize a hopelessly impossible dream, and in this sense proved themselves supremely unrealistic. "The United States," Kolko declared, "could not obtain that single prerequisite it had fixed as its goals—stability of the world economic and political order." In point of fact, concluded Kolko, "Stability was not for the Russians or anyone else to give or deny, for the war had shaken and shattered the world, and before anyone could chart its new course much would yet occur. For the war was the beginning of a world revolution which one could see everywhere, and the diplomats could not bargain over that, but simply hold one another responsible for the chaos they themselves helped to create."

Nonetheless, Kolko concluded that United States foreign policy should bear the burden for starting the Cold War. "In the final analysis," wrote Kolko of Cold War responsibility, "Washington's function was not to understand the character and needs of Russian policy but only the interests of the United States, and the large majority of American leaders considered it better to attain them crudely than not at all." Toward this end, and in a manner to suggest that the causes of the Cold War were basically economic, Kolko maintained that "American foreign policy at the end of World War II necessitated

the ability and desire to employ loans, credits and invest-
ments everywhere, to create a world economic order
according to its own needs and objectives, as the British
had done before in an earlier period." The argument
continued: "It is this deliberate quality, this articulate
set of economic and political goals which ultimately set
the United States at the end of World War II against the
Soviet Union, against the tide of the Left, and against
Britain as a coequal guardian of world capitalism—in
fact against history as it had been and had yet to
become."

Like Alperovitz and LaFeber, Kolko, in addition,
suggested that there was nothing accidental or adventitious about the formulation of post-World War II United
States foreign policy: "That there was something accidental or unintended about the American response to the
world is a comforting reassurance to those who wish to
confuse American rhetoric and description of intentions
[almost all idealistic] with the realities and purposes of
operational power." For Kolko, United States foreign
policy derived rationally and logically from an inherently
expansionistic capitalist political economy, whose structural dynamics required ever-expanding markets for
America's ever-growing surplus goods and capital, presumably in a freely trading open door world. One could
expect no less from such a singularly self-interested external outlook. In Kolko's words, "Given the society and
its needs American foreign policy could hardly have been
different." In this sense, the United States willed the Cold
War. Only a differently based political economy—perhaps a nonexpanding self-sufficient, democratic socialism
—could have made a difference.[79]

In *Architects of Illusion* (1970), the fourth and last
major New Left interpretation of the Cold War under
consideration, Lloyd C. Gardner advanced the thesis:
"There was a growing feeling in the early 1950's that

while Russia was obviously responsible for most of the evil in the world, American mistakes and shortcomings had brought on the Cold War." Gardner's study, whose general assumptions resembled those found in William Appleman Williams's earlier *Tragedy of American Diplomacy*, suggested "that the United States was more responsible for the *way* in which the Cold War developed."

The subject of responsibility dominated the discussion of postwar American-Soviet relations. Soviet fears, according to Gardner, were real and substantial. To the Soviet Union, he wrote, "American foreign policy after the war had been spearheaded by a military view of the world." Indeed, "All physical points of contact were military: Austria, Korea, Germany, Venezia Giula, Iran, Japan, China, and Manchuria." He opined, in a manner almost always missing from orthodox accounts of the Cold War, "Russia could not assume that America would use its technological and scientific advantages in purely defensive purposes." Pressures such as these inevitably produced a hardening on both sides.[80]

Despite emphasis on mutual suspicion, Gardner rejected the "tragic predicament" motif that informed the general approach of moderate revisionists such as Louis J. Halle. "To argue . . . that American Cold War policy or Soviet policy was simply part of an action-reaction syndrome in which one side or the other was totally justified, or for which neither side was responsible (as former Cold Warriors now argue) oversimplifies the matter." On the contrary, he argued, it is a fact of the first order that "responsibility for the *way* in which the Cold War developed, at least, belongs more to the United States." Gardner reached this conclusion by belaboring the obvious, or at least what seemed obvious to him. He wrote that at the end of the war, the United States had much greater opportunity and far more options to influence the course of events than the Soviet Union, whose situation in victory was worse in some ways than that of the defeated countries. By implication the United States could have avoided the Cold War altogether had it followed a more enlightened policy.[81]

Franklin Roosevelt's insistence on the United Nations Organization, for example, proved a mistake of considerable importance. By the time of the Yalta meeting Roosevelt no longer was in a position to dominate the Coalition. Nonetheless at Yalta he pushed for the creation of an international organization, which was expected to do for an American-led open door world what Wilson's League was to have done. Roosevelt never fully recognized, continued Gardner, that "the only way to make this new League work was to have reached prior agreement on issues left by the war itself, and hope that postwar questions could be handled as they arose." Pursuing the goal of a freely trading world, which Soviet perception of its own interests and needs never would have allowed, the President missed his only opportunity to create a stable postwar world. Hence the paradox that "while the United Nations was designed to be a peace-keeping device . . . it could not be made into a peace-keeping device without dividing the Big Three."

Truman, too, had little to offer the Soviets in the way of *quid pro quos,* presumably the only realistic basis upon which one could expect compromise with the Soviet Union. Truman, according to Gardner, instead "wanted to teach the Russians that they had to play their part in the new world order, and he wanted to do it by making it clear that America did not need Russian markets." In fact, the only policy that interested Truman, and Roosevelt before him, was the reconstruction and rationalization of a world economic order conducive to narrowly defined American needs. The subsequent Truman Doctrine and Marshall Plan only could be understood in this light. Americans pressed for their own program because they perceived that if the open door should fail to materialize in Europe "ultimately the American system of free enterprise would be endangered." What was at stake was nothing less than the free enterprise system at home: a political economy which, wrongly for the New Left, identified its prosperity and well-being with expansion abroad, i.e. locating markets for its vast industrial and capital surpluses. By arguing that a different political economy would have produced a different and hopefully less antagonist foreign policy, and by arguing that foreign policy would not change unless domestic institutions and traditions were reordered, the New Left urged the replacement of America's capitalist political economy with a self-sufficient nonexpanding society, presumably for most new revisionists, an autarkic democratic socialism. According to this analysis men may indeed make mistakes in the formulation and execution of foreign policy, the principal interpretive motif shared by Realist and conventional critics of modern American foreign policy. But to the New Left, in the words of Alperovitz, "the 'system' sets the terms of the issues" that policy makers decide. (In fact, so persuaded is Alperovitz that United States foreign policy is derived directly from America's political economy that he has ceased his research of foreign policy in order to concentrate "almost exclusively with domestic policy matters and with efforts to transform the political economy of our domestic institutions.")

To speak of mistakes or overly "legalistic-moralistic" approaches to international problems apart from the system in which they are generated, according to the new revisionism, was to ignore the essence of American foreign policy, the intimate and profound relationships between domestic and foreign policy.[82]

Returning to Gardner's analysis, the author suggested that any one of three foreign policy alternatives could have changed the course of post-World War II American

diplomacy, and in so doing "might have spared the world
the worst moments of the Cold War." First, wrote Gardner, there was "the way in which the question of economic aid for the Soviet Union was handled." Abrupt
termination of Lend-Lease, the failure to extend postwar
loans and credits, in fact, the utter American disregard
of obvious Soviet concern for rebuilding war-damaged
Russia, which could have been the basis for postwar
understanding and friendships, all contributed to dete-
riorating American-Soviet relations.

Second, he continued, there was "the failure to offer
the Soviets the guarantee of a German disarmament and
security treaty in early 1945." Had this been done, the
threat of "atomic diplomacy" and a German revival, a
problem of no small moment to Stalin, might have evapo-
rated amid a general feeling of goodwill and friendship.
Third, wrote Gardner, there was "the decision to pursue
the Baruch plan in the United Nations rather than Stimson's proposal to approach the Soviets directly on the
matter of controlling atomic energy." The obvious long-
term advantage of such a plan should have suggested
itself. Having done none of these things, the United States
harvested its crop of Soviet ill will.

In the end the United States opted for the open door
rather than what justifiably should have been considered
a Soviet sphere of interest in Eastern Europe. According
to the logic implicit in this nation's determination to
pursue a policy of industrial imperialism, "the world,"
reasoned Gardner, "could not be divided without being
closed to someone, so it had better not be divided." The
new revisionism reduced the complexity of the Cold War
to a single issue: America wanted an open door, and, as
Gardner concluded in a related context, "Russia did
not." Herein America started the Cold War.[83]

5. NEW LEFT DIPLOMATIC LITERATURE, 1960-1970

A Tentative Estimate

An attempt to determine the significance of the New Left diplomatic literature that began to emerge in the 1960's poses several problems which inhere in any effort to isolate and evaluate an historiographic trend in mid-stream. For example, whether New Left diplomatic historians will continue to emphasize the economic element of their current analyses during the decade of the 1970's remains a question that only can be answered at a later date. It seems likely that several of them will de-emphasize economic considerations, at least as determinative, will regain a sense of proportion, and will return to a more balanced multicausational interpretation of American diplomacy. Others, such as Kolko, probably will not.

What the student of historiography can do, however, in making a tentative evaluation of the significance of the new revisionism in the 1960's, is canvass the opinion of various well-known and respected practitioners in the

104

field of United States diplomatic history. These may be regarded as leading exponents of conventional or orthodox interpretations against which the new revisionism in part was supposed to have reacted. In this manner one can roughly estimate the impact of the New Left on the history academy as a whole. The purpose of these concluding remarks is to survey opinions, both published and unpublished, of a number of recognized scholars whose own works represent what the historical profession terms significant contributions to the literature of the subject.

In their published comments, traditional historians uniformly objected to the New Left tendency to distort the acquisitive element implicit in the admittedly economic motives of American entrepreneurs and government throughout the nation's history. "The quite natural desire of American businessmen to retain and expand foreign markets, and the role of the American government, like that of other governments, in furthering business interests abroad," wrote diplomatic historian Daniel M. Smith in 1969, "somehow became at revisionist hands 'economic imperialism,' 'open-door empire,' 'informal empire,' or some equally perjorative term." There was, according to the orthodox view, nothing inherently evil or sinister about the United States promoting its businessmen abroad or attempting to obtain equality of commercial opportunity for American citizens in other lands. What also disturbed the traditionalists was the New Left tendency to subordinate or omit altogether non-economic motives in the formulation of United States foreign policy. "Cultural, moral, humanitarian, and nationalist factors," commented Smith on the basically monocausational approach of the New Left, "are slighted or ignored entirely by such a determinist interpretation of history, and above all the capacity of man for merely irrational acts is passed over in silence." With such a one-dimensional view of human nature, he continued, "Apparently it cannot be allowed that a Hay, a Wilson, or an F.D.R., may genuinely have believed that freer world trade was beneficial to all countries nor that the nation has ever been moved by noble or generous impulses."

Smith, like many other observers of the new revisionism, distinguished New Left histories and historians from one another. He has written of Williams: "In fairness, Williams does recognize some of these factors, though he emphasizes the economic; it is some of his followers who have been more dogmatic." Smith, at times, reached diametrically opposed conclusions regarding the importance of various New Left monographs. Although he could find little of value in Gabriel Kolko's *The Roots of American Foreign Policy* (1969), he found N. Gordon Levin's *Woodrow Wilson and World Politics* (1968), despite some qualifications, a significant contribution to a better understanding of American diplomacy in World War I. What was the significance of the New Left? Like other traditional historians, Smith concluded that however one viewed the corpus of New Left diplomatic literature, which was by the nature of its preoccupation with economic considerations defective, revisionism's greatest value lay in its therapeutic influence on the historical profession. "This scholarly dialectical process," concluded Smith, "has not been unfortunate from the standpoint of historical knowledge, as new evidence and new interpretations have compelled a re-thinking of the past"; and "even the more extreme revisionism often has had some merit in the shaping of more intellectually satisfying historical syntheses."[84]

In a collection of transcribed conversations with historians compiled by John A. Garraty, Ernest R. May noted that the New Left's principal characteristics were economic determinism and excessive preoccupation with responsibility, the characteristics that ultimately placed the revisionism of the twenties and thirties outside the mainstream of American diplomatic historiography. The New Left emphasized "the way in which economic interests of individuals, groups, and corporations affect government policy", May wrote, and equally important, the New Left tended "to sit in judgment on the past and to write in terms of great mistakes that have been made, or villanies that have been perpetrated." Nonetheless, May was keenly interested in the new revisionism's belief in an alternative *Weltanschauung* as a framework for changing motivation from the supposedly business-dominated one that informed the bulk of New Left literature. More specifically, he explained, there was "the idea . . . that it is possible to create other models in which other sets of ideas—other sets of values than those of a business civilization—might have prevailed and produced a different course of conduct." May reflected on the whole, however, a rather negative attitude toward the New Left.[85]

In the same collection of conversations Robert H. Ferrell observed: "In the sense that all history is revisionism, I think we need these new interpretations or investigations." Conceding that, he then took exception to the New Left's approach, theses and motives. "In so far as the New Left has looked at foreign policy," wrote Ferrell, "they have read the present, especially the problem of Vietnam, into the past," and, as already noted by May, "they are concerned mainly with the mistakes of American policy." Ferrell suggested furthermore that the recent plethora of historical materials and the nature of graduate school training may have willy-nilly contributed to revisionist historiography in the 1960's. "The young historian," he wrote, "just coming out of graduate school, terribly anxious for a book, or at least an article, wanting something which will advance his fortune in the profession . . . the young historian, having been told by his graduate teachers that he must have an idea or thesis, and having learned also that it is possible to plunge into the morass of research materials and come out with something resembling support of almost any thesis, can put together a rather convincing, or at least plausible, argument which may not have much relation to history as it happened." In this sense, Ferrell implied that for some ambitious young scholars revisionism was a way of getting ahead. Ferrell also was persuaded that "worried about America's moral stature and distrusting the present government," the new Left "produced literature based largely on this type of material." Although Ferrell himself recognized the problem involved in reading all the historical materials available on a given subject, he contended that his criticism, and by inference his estimate of the significance, of the New Left rested on solid ground. "I think," he concluded unequivocally, "the New Left . . . tried to score points, set up their objectives, and then simply move flippantly into the archives for support."[86]

The remaining reaction to New Left diplomatic historiography contained in the Garraty collection was that of Richard W. Leopold. After observing that every historian's writings in part reflect his own experience and the climate of opinion in which he grew up, Leopold scored several aspects of New Left attitudes and assumptions that particularly bothered him. "What bothers me most," wrote Leopold in a manner suggestive of his dissatisfaction with the new revisionism, "is the assumption that, somehow, taking a position is more important than the documentary foundation on which the position rests and the thoroughness of the research . . . What is important to the New Left is to expose and to say something

new . . . A second attitude of the New Left that bothers
me," he continued, "is its intolerance—the assumption
that these matters are not susceptible to doubt." The
third New Left irritant to Leopold was the possibility
that a number of New Left historians writing in the field
of foreign policy were engaged in areas outside of their
competence. Specifically he cited "the tendency for New
Left writers who are interested in intellectual history
[Christopher Lasch? Gabriel Kolko?] to get themselves
involved in matters of foreign policy, which is really
outside their professional competence." In short, Leopold
found the New Left wanting.[87]

Among unpublished opinions of the new revisionism
by other traditional scholars which recently were col-
lected by the writer, prominent historian Thomas A.
Bailey noted that "as far as the New Left relates to
American diplomatic history, the main efforts seem to
be to overstress economic motivation (as did Beard) and
to find the United States rather than Soviet Russia primarily responsible for the Cold War." What impression,
if any, did this literature have on Bailey? "These writings," declared Bailey categorically, "have made scant
impact on me." This was for two essential reasons. "As
for economic motivation," wrote Bailey, "I have long
held that all relevant motives should be carefully
weighed, and that no one should be beaten to death or
found where it did not exist." For example, "To argue
that the United States forced the Cold War on Russia
primarily [Bailey's italics] because of a thirst for the
open door trade of Eastern Europe (it constituted about
one percent of our total exports) is nonsense." Who then
started the Cold War? Bailey suggested that basically
"both sides are to blame in the sense that their systems
are inherently antipathetical and react upon another" although he had not the slightest admiration for the Soviet

system of government. He concluded, "I do not regard much of the New Left [diplomatic historiography] as significant," because it is at bottom "poor scholarship." It was significant in a backhanded sense, however. Its significance, wrote Bailey, lay in the fact "that it stirs up controversy and will necessitate many more books, as was true of Beard, to get us back on the right track." Lamenting the increasing number of younger students being seduced by the new revisionism, he said it was indeed unfortunate that the New Left could be recognized as a unified school of thought. "All this means," wrote Bailey, "is that they start with a built-in bias, which is the very thing we were all warned against in graduate school." Bailey's comments placed him squarely against the new revisionism.

Historian Julius W. Pratt, a contemporary of Bailey, expressed a different and somewhat more favorable judgment. Pratt wrote that his "acquaintance with the New Left diplomatic historians is confined chiefly to their treatment of World War II and the Cold War, though I know they have given attention to other periods." Unlike Bailey, Pratt did not perceive the New Left as a monolithic school of thought. "Among those of whose work I know something," remarked Pratt, "there is so much diversity that it is impossible to categorize them as a group," inasmuch as "they range all the way from the careful scholars to a 'lunatic fringe' whose members see no virtue in the United States and no evil in the Soviet Union."

The former group apparently made a strong impression on Pratt. "Taking the more responsible of them," commented Pratt, "I should certainly say that their contribution is significant." To what extent were they significant? "They have shown," he continued, "that, contrary to the conventional view, the motives of the United States were not always unselfish or its suspicions of the Soviet Union always justified; that American statesmen did not always appreciate the needs, problems, and fears of the Soviet Union; that there may have been opportunities for accommodations in the early phases of the Cold War that we did not recognize." Pratt then qualified his statement: "All this can be granted without going all the way with even the more moderate of the group." In the end, he concluded philosophically, "it seems to me that we have an instance of the classic Hegelian thesis and antithesis, with the prospect that if we are lucky and survive so long, we may get a synthesis that will be rather generally acceptable." Pratt thus accepted some of the New Left's evidence and interpretation while rejecting its metaphysics, that is, the way in which New Lefters perceived and explained reality.

Herbert Feis, unlike Pratt, had little use for either New Left evidence or interpretations, both of which he found basically faulty. He found "the work of those New Left historians that I have read very unsatisfactory." By means of illustration he noted he "thought Alperovitz's *Atomic Diplomacy* (1965) careless and unscrupulous in the use of his sources, and his interpretation of the causes and background of events partisan and unsupported by the evidence." He further added, "William Appleman Williams's work has the same defects but has an even more Marxian bent." So far as Gabriel Kolko's *Politics of War* (1968) was concerned, Feis wrote, "I could not read beyond the first one hundred twenty pages because I found his writing too opaque." From another perspective, he continued, Kolko's study "seemed to me rather like a lot of index cards just strung together, each with its separate fragment of fact linked by generalizations that were doubtful; and supported by footnotes containing a whole cluster of references, so that it was impossible

to tell the precise source on which he based his opinion."
In fact, Feis doubted that New Left literature was scholarship at all. "Their books," he judged, "are to be regarded more in the nature of political tracts than a detailed historical examination."

What significance the New Left had, according to Feis,
lay in its immense influence on "the opinion of so many
younger writers about international affairs in the univer-
sities or as book reviews." In these areas New Left monographs fell on fertile soil, for reasons that are not too
difficult to understand. "Obviously," wrote Feis, "the
acceptance of the defective works of the historians of the
New Left by so many of the younger historians indicates
deep resentment and criticism about the conduct of
American foreign policy and military policy during the
past decade, especially the diplomatic and military mis-
judgment about the sad war in Vietnam, and tardy recognition of the influence of the military industrial complex." Feis, like Bailey, found it unfortunate that the
New Left could be recognized as a single school of interpretation, in his words "a singular identity not only of
opinions but in many cases also in language, often leav-
ing the impression that they are parroting each other." It
is extremely doubtful that Feis would have altered his
opinion of the New Left had he lived longer.

Turning to an historian whose special field of interest
is early twentieth-century American diplomacy, Bradford Perkins directed his comments about the New Left
directly toward Williams. "If, as I suppose," wrote
Perkins, "you consider William A. Williams a prime example of the 'New Left,' I would say that I consider his
Tragedy [*of American Diplomacy* (1959, rev. 1962)]
to be one of the most thought-provoking works we have
had in a long time." Nonetheless, he noted, "I think in
this book, as in those by other authors I would consider

'New Left,' Williams tends to confuse rhetoric with policy and also fails to recognize the fact that, in advocating
'open-door imperialism,' Americans can honestly feel
that they are not only serving the interests of their country but also those with whom they trade." Perkins found
Williams's *The Root of the Modern American Empire*
(1969) lacking for essentially similar reasons. "These
same failings," wrote Perkins, "are visible in *Roots,* where
Williams shows us a great deal of evidence of concern
and almost no evidence of effective policy." In particular, he explained, "I note how belated and how essentially
forceless was, for example, the American reaction to the
European restrictions on the importation of American
pork." Further confusion resulted from "Williams's casual
mingling of movements for territorial and commercial
expansion among American agriculturalists, a mingling
which marks the fact that these thrusts are not only different but often opposed." What then, if any, was Williams's and the New Left's significance? "Williams and
many others seem to me to make a great deal of sense
when they remind us of the steady American interest in
trade and of the capitalist-republican value system of this
country," but he concluded, "I have not been convinced
that these men make a very good case concerning specific
policies, except when, as in the case of the episodes examined by Thomas McCormick [*China Market* (1967)]
and other similar cases, they are harrowing rather familiar ground." Bradford Perkins's reaction to the New Left
was mixed.

Dexter Perkins, the father of Bradford Perkins, an
eminent scholar and a staunch opponent of revisionism,
viewed the work of the New Left in a more doubtful
light. Perkins suggested that much of the New Left literature, especially those works concerned with the Cold
War, proceeded from hypotheses which he at best con-

sidered dubious. The New revisionism wrongly assumed that gestures of conciliation "from the United States will be met by conciliation on the other side," hence, adding, "this is a gratuitous assumption." He went on to say that the New Left wrongly assumed "that purposes of the Communist states, which can, of course, be explained in terms of their own ideology, rest upon the same moral basis as the purposes of the West." Most important, ended Perkins, the New Left erroneously assumed "that the international discourse [of nations] is based on rationality, whereas it really rests upon a conflict of interests, ideals and considerations of prestige." From this standpoint, the new revisionism seems to have had slight impact on Dexter Perkins.

Robert E. Osgood similarly disapproved of the New Left. Osgood judged that on the whole New Left historians "are generally incompetent historians," with the notable exceptions of Williams, Kolko and Lloyd C. Gardner. Osgood also found the New Left's reliance on economic considerations misplaced. "Their economic determinism," he observed in a way indicating his distaste for the new trend, "is quite inadequate to explain reality but does explain a good deal about the psychology of American liberal protests throughout history." Was the New Left significant? While not denying that it has exerted some influence, presumably at least on younger historians and the radical political left, Osgood predicted that "their influence will be much less than that of the post-World War I revisionists."

Robert A. Divine's response to the New Left was an admixture of praise and criticism. "My reaction to the New Left historians," explained Divine, "is favorable but critical, favorable in the sense that I think a reassessment of such issues as the origins of the Cold War was long overdue, but critical in the sense that their ideological bias frequently distorts their conclusions." Divine suggested that when speaking of the New Left, one must distinguish between the revisionist historians: "I think it is a mistake to lump all of the so-called New Left historians together." Under closer examination, he explained, "Some are much more scholarly in their use of evidence than others, and some are much more balanced in their approach and argument than their colleagues." In fact, he concluded, "Most New Left historians today deny that they form a tightly knit school and stress their own internal differences."

Focusing mainly on new revisionism's contribution to Cold War literature, Forrest C. Pogue expressed a somewhat positive view of the New Left. "Certainly," wrote Pogue, "the work of the New Left scholars on diplomacy is significant" to the extent that "they ask for a re-examination of early assumptions [implicit in the formulation of post-World War II American foreign policy] and point to different conclusions." Pogue often disagreed with them, however. "On the basis of those documents which I have examined in the Pentagon and the State Department," wrote Pogue, "I often do not agree with their conclusions," having particularly serious reservation about the research of Kolko and Alperovitz. "Nonetheless," he concluded, "the questions should be asked." Herein lay the special contribution of the new revisionism.

Surprisingly, in that most of his previous comments regarding the new revisionism were adversely critical, political scientist Hans J. Morgenthau observed that his overall reaction to the New Left was "positive." To begin with, he noted, "I do not think one can pass summary judgment on the New Left diplomatic historians," for, as has been recognized by the majority of traditional historians discussed, "some are good as historians, others are not." One had to differentiate the dogmatic element from the more sophisticated. In this light, he continued, "Some are useful because they look at historic events from a new perspective, others are not because they allow their philosophical preconceptions to interfere with their assessment of this historic evidence." The significance of the New Left, according to Morgenthau, lay mostly in its ability to stimulate debate. Because historic evidence has for so long been interpreted almost exclusively from the official, orthodox view, he finished, "I find it healthy to look at it from a different, equally legitimate and equally partial point of view."

Norman A. Graebner expressed much the same sentiment. "I know many of the New Left historians very well," wrote Graebner, "and have a high regard for them, but I do not always accept their ideas." For example, he explained, "They tend to distort . . . by making too much of too little material." He put it in another, more earthy manner: "When one goes through a forest, does one follow the big tracks or run off looking for broken twigs?" In this sense, he added, "who is guilty of oversimplification is not clear." Graebner himself has followed the "big tracks."

"I happen," wrote Graebner, "much as Daniel Smith, to concentrate on what I regard to be the major thrust of policy and opinion." Contrary to the traditional approach, "The New Left tends to search for side issues and side, almost imperceptible, pressures," all of which are very difficult to prove in making a case for an economic theory of causation. Yet Graebner regarded the New Left diplomatic historiography of the 1960's as a significant contribution to the literature of American diplomacy. "I regard the New Left important—very important," he wrote. "In that group are some very able, hard-working and extremely honest historians. They see the country engaging in policies and wonder why." What is the explanation? "Can this be the result of unclear thinking? political pressures? a bad reading of history by officials? or economic pressures and needs to keep the American economy rolling with overseas trade and investment?"

While not denying the presence of economic considerations in foreign policy decision-making, Graebner contended that from his vantage point non-economic considerations outweighed them. He said, "I believe that the Polish Americans had more influence on Cold War decisions than businessmen regarding Eastern Europe." Although he asked the same question as the New Left, i.e., "Why the everlasting overcommitment?" Graebner concluded that explanations of American foreign policy must in the final analysis be attributed "to political and intellectual causes, not economic." He noted of the new revisionism, "What the New Left has done is to join many of the rest of us in examining the record." And that is commendable. According to Graebner, the New Left produced "evidence and ideas that cannot be refuted and thus make their contribution." The history academy has room for many opinions. "I feel," he ended, "there is room for historians of all schools provided that all are honest. Eventually we will all benefit as we see more clearly what has happened and why."

What these scholarly commentators might have to say about the New Left in 1981 would be as difficult to predict as would be predicting the course New Left historians will take during the coming decade. At that time it would be interesting to canvass the opinions of the same men, or at least an equally representative sample, and compare their evaluations. From the critical examination of the new revisionism provided in this analysis, and from comments, published and unpublished, of traditional historians, however, one can draw a number of tentative conclusions concerning the significance of the New Left diplomatic literature that began to appear in the 1960's. Traditional historians, on the basis of opinions contained here, found the New Left significant to the extent that it compelled a reassessment of the past and a reexamination of historical source materials. In this manner the impact of the New Left on the history academy had a backhanded quality.

Traditional historians also found diversity among New Left diplomatic historians. They discerned among the New Left a group of extremist historians who adhered more or less exclusively to an economic interpretation of American diplomatic history. Typical of this group was Gabriel Kolko. They discerned another group of comparatively more sophisticated and balanced New Lefters who, while placing great weight on economic considerations, adhered to a relatively multicausational interpretation of American foreign policy. For example, it could be argued that Levin's views flowed logically from the work of "semi-realistic" writers such as Edward H. Buehrig, Ernest R. May and Daniel M. Smith on World War I insofar as they depicted United States ideals and self-interests as more harmonized than previously perceived in Wilsonian diplomacy. In earlier works, furthermore, there was much less explicit reference by policy makers to economic considerations than Levin maintained was the case. Parrini's study of Wilsonian foreign policy fell into the same category. Gardner's thesis concerning the relationship between what he contended to be the essentially economic nature of New Deal diplomacy and American entry into World War II similarly could be said to have derived from earlier works that stressed the total challenge of totalitarianism both to American ideals and self-interest. These illustrations suggest that a reasonable synthesis can be defended, drawing from the work of moderate revisionists on the one side and certain traditional historians on the other. Whatever may be said of the relative merits of individual revisionist monographs, there could be no question that traditional historians on the whole rejected the main thrust of New Left scholarship. Practitioners of orthodox history rejected outright the New Left contention that United States foreign policy could be explained as an ongoing and direct function of the nation's capitalist political economy. Traditional historians denied, moreover, that American foreign policy derived rationally and logically from an inherently expansionist political economy whose structural requirements demanded ever-expanding foreign markets and sources of raw materials for America's ever-growing surplus goods and capital, all in a stable, liberal-minded and freely trading open door world. To have accepted such a thesis would in effect have deprived American diplomatic history of much of its accidental and adventitious quality, not to mention the strong sense of idealism and humanitarianism that has informed much of United States foreign policy. Finally, to suggest as did New Left diplomatic historians, that human behavior is essentially rational and powered by motives that are primarily economic seemed strangely anachronistic in the second half of the twentieth century. To approach the generally recognized complexity of reality with such a simple and simplistic tool of understanding said, one suspected, a great deal more about its possessor than about historical causation. In sum, much of the New Left diplomatic historiography that emerged in the 1960's lacked intellectual validity.

NOTES

1. Smith, "The New Left and the Cold War," p. 79.
2. *Ibid.* Cohen, *The American Revisionists,* p. 2.
3. Schlesinger, "Origins of the Cold War," p. 23. Johnson, "The New Generation of Isolationists," pp. 138–39.
4. Bernstein, "Towards a New Past," ix. Kolko, *The Roots of American Foreign Policy,* p. 9. *The Politics of War,* pp. 166, 245, 249. LaFeber, *America, Russia, and the Cold War, 1945–1966,* p. 195.
5. Nearing, *The American Empire; The Tragedy of Empire.* P. M. S. Blackett, *Military and Political Consequences of Atomic Energy,* p. 127. Alperovitz, *Atomic Diplomacy.* Adler and Patterson, "Red Fascism," p. 1046. K. Zilliacus, *Mirror of the Past,* ix.
6. Morgenthau, *Scientific Power vs. Power Politics,* pp. 9–10, 201–202. Historians representative of the Realist outlook include, among others, Norman Graebner, Herbert Feis, M. F. Herz, and Louis J. Halle.
25.
7. Morgenthau, *In Defense of National Interest,* pp. 23,
8. Morgenthau, "The Mainsprings of American Foreign Policy," p. 853; *In Defense of National Interest,* p. 160.

9. Kennan, *American Diplomacy, 1900–1950*, pp. 82–83.

10. *Ibid.*, pp. 16, 21–22, 35.

11. *Ibid.*, pp. 58, 62.

12. *Ibid.*, p. 68; *Realities of American Foreign Policy*, pp. 26–27.

13. Tannenbaum, *The American Tradition in Foreign Policy*, p. 168.

14. Williams, *The Roots of the Modern American Empire*, p. 426. LaFeber, *The New Empire*, vii. McCormick, *China Market*, p. 100; Gardner, "American Foreign Policy, 1900–1921," pp. 203–204, 226.

15. Levin, *Woodrow Wilson and World Politics*, viii. Parrini, *Heir to Empire*, pp. 13–14.

16. Gardner, *Economic Aspects of New Deal Diplomacy*, p. 98. (Gardner's Italics) Robert Freeman Smith, "American Foreign Relations, 1920–42," p. 237. Horowitz, *Empire and Revolution*, p. 234. Gardner, *Architects of Illusion*, x, pp. 317–18. (Gardner's Italics) Kolko, *The Politics of War*, p. 486. LaFeber, *America, Russia, and the Cold War*, p. 6. Kolko, *The Roots of American Foreign Policy*, p. 85.

17. Williams, *The Contours of American History*, p. 490. LaFeber, "The Conscious Creation of a World Wide Empire," review of *The Rising American Empire* by R. W. Van Alstyne, in *Studies on the Left, II (1962)*, p. 103. Beard, *The Devil Theory of War*, pp. 120–21.

18. Williams, *The Roots of the Modern American Empire*, xx–xxi.

19. Williams, *The Contours of American History*, p. 19; "The Frontier Thesis and American Foreign Policy," p. 395; *The Tragedy of American Diplomacy*, p. 307.

20. Hofstadter, "Manifest Destiny and the Philippines," p. 198. Williams, *The Contours of American History*, pp. 20–21.

21. *Ibid.*, pp. 222, 365, 374; *The Great Expansion*, 12.

22. *Ibid.*, pp. 48, 75, 83. (Williams's italics)

23. Williams, *The Roots of the Modern American Empire*, xiii.

24. Williams, *American-Russian Relations, 1781–1947*, pp. 23, 47. McCormick, *China Market*, p. 192.

25. Williams, *American-Russian Relations, 1781–1947,* pp. 95, 105, 159, 163; *The Tragedy of American Diplomacy,* p. 83.

26. Perkins, *The Diplomacy of a New Age,* p. 18.

27. Williams, *American-Russian Relations, 1781–1947,* pp. 259, 263, 270. (Williams's italics)

28. *Ibid.,* p. 270.

29. Williams, *The Roots of the Modern American Empire,* xiii–xvi.

30. Williams, *The Tragedy of American Diplomacy,* pp. 292, 303.

31. *Ibid.,* pp. 29–30; *The Roots of the Modern American Empire,* pp. 408–409, 425–26. (Williams's italics)

32. Williams, *The Great Evasion,* p. 42; *The Tragedy of American Diplomacy,* p. 47.

33. *Ibid.,* pp. 81, 159.

34. *Ibid.,* pp. 205–206. (Williams's italics)

35. *Ibid.,* pp. 206–208. (Williams's italics)

36. *Ibid.,* pp. 303, 307.

37. Williams, *The United States, Cuba, and Castro,* pp. 19, 139.

38. *Ibid.,* pp. 139–40, 160.

39. Williams, "Rise of an American World Power Complex," p. 1.

40. LaFeber, *The New Empire,* vii, ix, p. 1.

41. *Ibid.,* pp. 6, 67, 69, 325.

42. *Ibid.,* pp. 379, 397, 401, 404.

43. *Ibid.,* pp. 408, 411–412, 416.

44. McCormick, *China Market,* pp. 9, 21–22, 233. (McCormick's italics)

45. *Ibid.,* pp. 22, 51–52. (McCormick's italics)

46. *Ibid.,* pp. 179, 185–86.

47. *Ibid.,* pp. 191–92, 197.

48. Levin, *Woodrow Wilson and World Politics,* vii, pp. 4, 8.

49. *Ibid.,* p. 34.

50. *Ibid.,* pp. 25–26.

51. Mayer, *Wilson vs. Lenin,* vii, pp. 35, 366.

52. Mayer, *Politics and Diplomacy of Peacemaking,* vii, p. 15.

53. Parrini, *Heir to Empire*, pp. 1, 10, 259. (Parrini's italics)

54. *Ibid.,* pp. 10, 13–14, 140–41.

55. *Ibid.,* pp. 138, 141.

56. Gardner, *Economic Aspects of New Deal Diplomacy*, vii, pp. 3, 154.

57. *Ibid.,* pp. 98, 329. (Gardner's italics)

58. Smith, "American Foreign Relations, 1920–42," pp. 237–38, 245.

59. Graebner, "Cold War Origins and the Continuing Debate," pp. 126–27. Feis, *Churchill, Roosevelt and Stalin*, pp. 483, 563. Jones, *The Fifteen Weeks*, p. 41. Ulam, *Expansion and Coexistence*, p. 377.

60. Butterfield, *History and Human Relations*, pp. 9–36. Halle, *The Cold War As History*, xiii. Perkins, *The Diplomacy of a New Age*, p. 34; *The American Approach to Foreign Policy*, p. 222.

61. Alperovitz, *Atomic Diplomacy*, p. 13; D. F. Fleming, *The Cold War and Its Origins*, I, p. 1045.

62. Alperovitz, *Cold War Essays*, pp. 30, 40, 109–110. (Alperovitz's italics)

63. *Ibid.,* p. 110. (Alperovitz's italics)

64. *Ibid.,* pp. 56–58.

65. *Ibid.,* pp. 56, 112–13, 144. (Alperovitz's italics)

66. *Ibid.,* pp. 227, 239–40. (Alperovitz's italics)

67. Kolko, *The Politicis of War*, pp. 38, 244, 349, 597, 602.

68. Gardner, *Architects of Illusion*, pp. 306–307.

69. LaFeber, *America, Russia, and the Cold War*, p. 2.

70. *Ibid.,* p. 6.

71. *Ibid.,* pp. 12, 14.

72. *Ibid.,* pp. 14–15.

73. *Ibid.,* p. 155.

74. Kolko, *The Politics of War*, pp. 3–4.

75. *Ibid.,* pp. 4–5.

76. *Ibid.,* p. 265.

77. *Ibid.,* pp. 245, 249, 252, 265, 621.

78. *Ibid.,* pp. 143, 164–65, 622.

79. *Ibid.,* pp. 368–69, 449, 624–25.

80. Gardner, *Architects of Illusion,* vii, x, p. 317. (Gardner's italics)

81. *Ibid.,* p. 317. (Gardner's italics)

82. *Ibid.,* pp. 52–53, 57–58, 227. Alperovitz, *Cold War Essays,* pp. 4, 91.

83. Gardner, *Architects of Illusion,* pp. 317–18, *Economic Aspects of New Deal Diplomacy,* p. 329. (Gardner's italics)

84. Smith, "The New Left and the Cold War," pp. 78, 81–82.

85. Garraty, *Interpreting American History,* II, pp. 92–93.

86. *Ibid.,* pp. 221, 226.

87. *Ibid.,* p. 244.

BIBLIOGRAPHY

For a general introduction to the New Left diplomatic literature of the 1960's one should begin with Irwin Unger, "The 'New Left' and American History: Some Recent Trends in United States Historiography," *American Historical Review,* LXXII (July, 1967), 1237-63; Daniel M. Smith, "The New Left and the Cold War," review of *Empire and Revolution: A Radical Interpretation of Contemporary World History,* by David Horowitz, in the *Denver Quarterly, IV* (Winter, 1970), 78-88; Arthur Schlesinger, Jr., "Origins of the Cold War," *Foreign Affairs,* XLVI (October, 1967), 22-52; Charles S. Maier, "Revisionism and the Interpretation of Cold War Origins," *Perspectives in American History,* VI (1970), 313-47; David Donald, "Radical Historians on the Move," *New York Times Book Review,* July 19, 1970, 1 ff; and James A. Johnson, "The New Generation of Isolationists," *Foreign Affairs,* XLIX (October, 1970), 136-46. Less balanced but also informative are Christopher Lasch, "The Cold War, Revisited and Revisioned," *New York Times Magazine*, January 14, 1968, 27 ff; Thomas J. McCormick, "The State of American Diplomatic History," in *The State of American History*, ed. by Herbert J. Bass (Chicago: Quadrangle Books, 1970); and James O'Brien *et al.*, "New Left Historian of the 1960's," *Radical America* (November, 1970), 81-106. Other important essays that appeared too late for inclusion into this study are Robert W. Tucker, *The Radical Left and American Foreign Policy* (Baltimore: Johns Hopkins Press, 1971); and *Twentieth-Century American Foreign Policy*, ed. by John Braeman, Robert H. Bremner and David Brody (Columbus, Ohio: Ohio State University Press, 1971).

The best account of World War I revisionism is Warren I. Cohen, *The American Revisionists: The Lessons of Intervention in World War I* (Chicago: University of Chicago Press, 1967). For a description of the nature of twentieth-century American diplomatic history see Richard W. Leopold, "The Problem of American Intervention, 1917: An Historical Retrospect," *World Politics*, II (April, 1950), 405-25; Wayne S. Cole, "American Entry into World War II: A Historiographical Appraisal," *Mississippi Valley Historical Review*, XLIII (March, 1957), 595-617; Daniel M. Smith, "National Interest and American Intervention, 1917: An Historiographical Appraisal," *Journal of American History*, LII (June, 1965), 5-24; Ernest R. May, "Emergence to World Power," in *The Reconstruction of American History*, ed. by John Higham (New York: Harper and Brothers, 1962), 180-96; and *American Intervention: 1917 and 1941* (2nd ed., Service Center for Teachers of History, Pamphlet 30, 1969).

For the debate surrounding "consensus" historiography see John Higham's "The Cult of the 'American Consensus': Homogenizing Our History," *Commentary,* XXVII (February, 1951), 93-100; and "Beyond Consensus: The Historian as Moral Critic," *American Historical Review,* LXVII (April, 1962), 609-25. A perceptive treatment of the connection between consensus history and United States diplomatic historiography is Francis L. Loewenheim's "A Legacy of Hope and a Legacy of Doubt: Reflections on the Role of History and Historians in American Foreign Policy since the Eighteenth Century," in *The Historian and the Diplomat: The Role of History and Historians in American Foreign Policy,* ed. by Francis L. Loewenheim (New York: Harper and Row, 1967).

Examples of earlier critics of United States foreign policy include Scott Nearing, *The American Empire* (New York: Rand School of Social Science, 1921); and *The Tragedy of Empire* (New York: Island Press, 1945); P. M. S. Blackett, *Military and Political Consequences of Atomic Energy* (London: Turnstile Press, 1948); K. Zilliacus, *Mirror of the Past: A History of Secret Diplomacy* (New York: Current Books, Inc., A. A. Wyn, 1946).

Comments on the Realist School of American foreign policy may be found in John Higham, Leonard Krieger and Felix Gilbert, *History: The Development of Historical Studies in the United States* (Englewood Cliffs, N. J.: Prentice-Hall, Inc., 1965); Donald Brandon, *American Foreign Policy: Beyond Utopianism and Realism* (New York: Appleton-Century-Crofts, 1966); Christopher Lasch, "The Historian as Diplomat," *Nation,* November 24, 1962, 348-53; and *The New Radicalism in America: The Intellectual as a Social Type* (New York: Vintage Books, 1965). For a better criticism of the Realist School consult Frank Tannenbaum, *The American Tradition in Foreign Policy* (Norman, Oklahoma: University of Oklahoma Press, 1955).

Hans J. Morgenthau's early postwar development can be traced in *Scientific Man vs. Power Politics* (Chicago: University of Chicago Press, 1946); and *In Defense of National Interest: A Critical Examination of American Foreign Policy* (New York: Alfred A. Knopf, 1952); and "The Mainsprings of American Foreign Policy: The National Interest vs. Moral Abstractions," *American Political Science Review,* XLIV (December, 1950), 833-54. For George F. Kennan see *American Diplomacy, 1900-1950* (New York: Mentor, 1951); *Realities of American Foreign Policy* (New York: W. W. Norton, Inc., 1954); *Memoirs, 1925-1950* (Boston: Little, Brown and Co., 1967).

The ideas of Charles A. Beard that most nearly parallel those of the New Left are contained in, among others, *Contemporary American History, 1877-1913* (New York: Macmillan Co., 1914); *The Open Door at Home: A Trial Philosophy of National Interest* (New York: Macmillan Co., 1934); *The Devil Theory of War: An Inquiry into the Nature of History and the Possibility of Keeping Out of War* (New York: Greenwood Press, 1936).

On the nature of the relationship between personality and the writing of history refer to Sidney Verba, "Assumptions of Rationality and Non-Rationality in Models of the International System," *World Politics,* XIV (October, 1961), 93-117; John D. Hicks, "The Personal Factor in the Writing of History," *Pacific Northwest Quarterly,* LV (July, 1964), 94-104; and Thomas J. Pressly, *Americans Interpret Their Civil War* (New York: Free Press, 1954). For a discussion of the revisionist mentality *per se* particularly useful are Dexter Perkins, *The American Approach to Foreign Policy* (rev. ed., Cambridge: Harvard University Press, 1962); and *Yield of the Years:*

An Autobiography (Boston: Little, Brown and Co., 1969).
Biographical data of William A. Williams are found in Joseph M. Siracusa, "New Left Diplomatic Histories and Historians: A Critical Examination of Recent Trends in American Diplomatic Historiography, 1960-1970," an unpublished Ph.D. dissertation, University of Colorado, 1971; and in Williams's *The Roots of the Modern American Empire: A Study of the Growth and Shaping of Social Consciousness in a Marketplace Society* (New York: Random House, 1969). Among Williams's published books and articles the most important are *The Contours of American History* (Chicago: Quadrangle Books, 1961); *The Great Evasion: An Essay on the Contemporary Relevance of Karl Marx and on the Wisdom of Admitting the Heretic into the Dialogue about America's Future* (Chicago: Quadrangle Books, 1964); *The Tragedy of American Diplomacy* (rev. and enl.; New York: Dell Publishing Co., Inc., 1962); *The United States, Cuba, and Castro: An Essay on the Dynamics of Revolution and the Dissolution of Empire* (New York: M [onthly] R [eview] Press, 1962); "Rise of an American World Power Complex," in *Struggle Against History: U.S. Foreign Policy in an Age of Revolution*, ed. by Neal D. Houghton (New York: Washington Square Press, 1968); "The Frontier Thesis and American Foreign Policy," *Pacific Historical Review*, XXIV (November, 1955), 379-95.

For C. Vann Woodward's call for the return of an "apocalyptic historiography" see "The Age of Reinterpretation," *American Historical Review* (October, 1964), 1-19. Notable non-New Left works that examine the nature of American expansionism in general and the role of land in particular are Arthur B. Darling, *Our*

Rising Empire, 1763-1803 (New Haven: Yale University Press, 1940); Gerald Stourzh, *Benjamin Franklin and American Foreign Policy* (Chicago: University of Chicago Press, 1954); Albert K. Weinberg, *Manifest Destiny: A Study of Nationalist Expansionism in American History* (Baltimore: Johns Hopkins University Press, 1935); Sylvester K. Stephens, *American Expansion in Hawaii, 1842-1898* (New York: Russell and Russell, 1945); Norman A. Graebner, *Empire on the Pacific: A Study in American Continental Expansion* (New York: Ronald Press Co., 1955); Frederick Merk and Lois B. Merk, *Manifest Destiny and Mission in American History: A Reinterpretation* (New York: Vintage Books, 1963).

The classic New Left study of the Spanish-American War and the ensuing imperialist vs. anti-imperialist debate is Walter LaFeber's *The New Empire: An Interpretation of American Expansion, 1860-1898* (Ithaca, New York: Cornell University Press for the American Historical Association, 1963). Less satisfying but fuller on agriculturists' positions is Williams's *The Roots of the Modern American Empire*. For a revisionist account of America's quest for overseas markets in general and China in particular see Thomas J. McCormick, *China Market: America's Quest for Informal Empire, 1893-1901* (Chicago: Quadrangle Books, 1967). A briefer and highly partisan development of this same theme is John W. Rollins, "The Anti-Imperialists and Twentieth-Century American Foreign Policy," *Studies on the Left,* III, (1962), 9-24. Also see Barton J. Bernstein and Franklin J. Leib, "Progressive Republican Senators and American Imperialism, 1898-1916: A Reappraisal," *Mid-America,* L (July, 1968), 163-205. Two important essays suggesting that the debate was in fact about fundamentals rather than tactics are Robert L. Beisner, *Twelve Against Em-*

pire: The Anti-Imperialists, 1898-1900 (New York: Holt Rinehart and Winston, 1965); and Berkeley E. Tompkins, *Anti-Imperialism in the United States: The Great Debate, 1890-1920* (Philadelphia: University of Pennsylvania Press, 1970). Treatment of the overproduction theme includes among others Ray Ginger, *Age of Excess: The United States from 1877 to 1914* (New York: Macmillan Co., 1965); Samuel P. Hays, *The Response to Industrialism: 1885-1914* (Chicago: University of Chicago Press, 1957); Foster Rhen Dulles, *America in the Pacific: A Century of Expansion* (Boston: Houghton Mifflin Co., 1952); Julius W. Pratt, *America's Colonial Experiment: How the United States Gained, Governed, and in Part Gave Away a Colonial Empire* (New York: Prentice-Hall, Inc., 1950).

Standard interpretations of the Spanish-American War regarding such factors as Social Darwinism, the perversion of Manifest Destiny, the psychic crisis of the 1890's and the influence of foreign examples on the nation's foreign policy public are found respectively in Julius W. Pratt, *Expansionists of 1898: The Acquisition of Hawaii and the Spanish Islands* (Gloucester, Mass.: Peter Smith, 1936); Merk and Merk, *Manifest Destiny and Mission in American History;* Richard Hofstadter, "Manifest Destiny and the Philippines," in *America in Crisis,* ed. by Daniel Aaron (New York: Alfred A. Knopf, 1952); and Ernest R. May, *American Imperialism: A Speculative Essay* (New York: Atheneum, 1968).

New Left works most directly concerned with the nature of Wilsonian diplomacy are N. Gordon Levin, *Woodrow Wilson and World Politics: America's Response to War and Revolution* (New York: Oxford University Press, 1968); Arno J. Mayer, *Wilson vs. Lenin: Political Origins of the New Diplomacy, 1917-1918* (Cleveland: World Publishing Co., 1959); *Politics and Diplomacy of Peacemaking: Containment and Counterrevolution at Versailles, 1918-1919* (New York: Alfred A. Knopf, 1967); and Carl P. Parrini, *Heir to Empire: United States Economic Diplomacy, 1916-1923* ([Pittsburgh:] University of Pittsburgh Press, 1969). Also see Lloyd C. Gardner's "American Foreign Policy 1900-1921: A Second Look at the Realist Critique of American Diplomacy," in *Towards a New Past: Dissenting Essays in American History,* ed. by Barton J. Bernstein (New York: Pantheon Books, 1968); Orde S. Pinckney, "William E. Borah: Critic of American Foreign Policy," *Studies on the Left,* I (1960), 48-61. For revisionist handling of the interwar period consult Lloyd C. Gardner's *Economic Aspects of New Deal Diplomacy* (Madison, Wisconsin: University of Wisconsin Press, 1965); and Robert Freeman Smith's shorter "American Foreign Relations, 1920-42," in *Towards a New Past: Dissenting Essays in American History,* ed. by Barton J. Bernstein (New York: Pantheon Books, 1968).

For background and the best available introduction to the Cold War literature refer to Norman A. Graebner, "Cold War Origins and the Continuing Debate," *Journal of Conflict Resolution,* XIII (Marsh, 1969), 123-32. Standard and moderate revisionists sources consulted include Herbert Feis, *Churchill, Roosevelt, Stalin: The War They Waged and the Peace They Sought* (Princeton: University Press, 1966); *The Atomic Bomb and the End of World War II* (rev. ed., Princeton: Princeton University Press, 1966); and *From Trust to Terror: The Onset of the Cold War, 1945-1950* (New York: W. W. Norton, Inc., 1970); Joseph M. Jones, *The Fifteen Weeks* (New York: Viking Press, 1955); Adam B. Ulam, *Expansion and Coexistence: The History of Soviet Foreign Policy, 1917-67* (New York: Frederick A. Prager, 1968); Dexter Perkins, *The Diplomacy of a New Age: Major Issues in U.S. Policy since 1945* (Bloomington, Indiana: Indiana University Press, 1967); and Louis J. Halle, *The Cold War as History* (New York: Harper and Row, 1967).

Major New Left interpretations of the Cold War are found in Gar Alperovitz, *Atomic Diplomacy: Hiroshima and Potsdam, The Use of the Atomic Bomb and the American Confrontation with Soviet Power* (New York: Vintage Books, 1965); *Cold War Essays* (Garden City, New York: Doubleday and Co., Inc., 1970); Lloyd C. Gardner, *Architects of Illusion: Men and Ideas in American Foreign Policy, 1941-1949* (Chicago: Quadrangle Books, 1970); Walter LaFeber, *America, Russia and the Cold War, 1945-1966* (New York: John Wiley and Sons, Inc. 1967); Gabriel Kolko, *The Politics of War: The World and United States Foreign Policy, 1943-1945* (New York: Vintage Books, 1968); *The Roots of American Foreign Policy: An Analysis of Power and Purpose* (Boston: Beacon Press, 1969); and David Horowitz, *Empire and Revolution: A Radical Interpretation of Contemporary World History* (New York: Vintage Books, 1969); *The Free World Colossus: A Critique of American Policy in the Cold War* (rev. ed., New York: Hall and Wang, 1971).

Of a large number of revisionist articles treating specific episodes the most important include Les K. Adler and Thomas G. Patterson, "Red Fascism: The Merger of Nazi Germany and Soviet Russia in the American Image of Totalitarianism, 1930's-1960's" *American Historical Review,* LXXV (April, 1970), 1046-64; David Geen, "The Cold War Comes to Latin America," in *Politics and Policies of the Truman Administration,* ed. by Barton J. Bernstein (Chicago: Quadrangle Books, 1970); Thomas G. Patterson, "The Quest for Peace and Prosperity: International Trade, Communism, and the Marshall Plan," in *ibid;* and "The Abortive Loan to Russia and the Origins of the Cold War, 1943-1946," *Journal of American History,* LVI (June, 1969), 79-92.

For an earlier, influential and clearly non-New Left critique of Truman's foreign policy, see D. F. Fleming's *The Cold War and Its Origins* (2 vols.; Garden City, New York: Doubleday and Co., Inc., 1961). For a corrective to New Left and other critical accounts of the alleged abrupt stoppage of Lend Lease to Russia, refer to George C. Herring, Jr., "Lend Lease to Russia and Origins of the Cold War, 1944-1945," *Journal of American History, LVI* (June, 1969), 93-114. Of the revisionist Cold War essays that appeared after this writing the most significant are Joyce Kolko and Gabriel Kolko, *The Limits of Power: The World and United States Foreign Policy, 1945-1954* (New York: Harper and Row, 1972); and Richard Barnet, *Roots of War* (New York: Atheneum, 1972).

Traditional diplomatic historians' reactions to the New Left may be obtained from the many book and essay reviews found in standard scholarly journals; John A. Garraty's *Interpreting American History: Conversations with Historians* (2 vols., New York: Macmillan Co., 1970); and from the previously cited Siracusa dissertation.

INDEX

Adler, Les K, 8
Alperovitz, Gar, 8, 80-86, 102-111, 115
Atkinson, Edward, 56

Bailey, Thomas A., 109-110
Beard, Charles Austin, 20-22, 27, 109-110
Bernstein, Barton J., 6
Bolshevik Revolution, 35
Boxer Rebellion, 61
Buehrig, Edward H., 118
Butterfield, Herbert, 77-78
Byrnes, James F., 86

Castro, Fidel, 47-48
Churchill, Winston, 11, 81
Cold War, 4-5, 11-12, 14-15, 19, 38-40, 45-46, 62, 76-103
"Consensus" historiography, 6

Divine, Robert A., 114-115

Farmer's Holiday Association, 24
Feis, Herbert, 76, 111-112
Ferrell, Robert H., 107-108
Fleming, D. F., 81
Four Point Program, 61